Law Essentials

D0257647

INTELLECTUAL PROPERTY LAW

Law Essentials

INTELLECTUAL PROPERTY LAW

Duncan Spiers, M.A. (Oxon)

Advocate;
Lecturer in Law, Napier University

DUNDEE UNIVERSITY PRESS
2009

First edition published in Great Britain in 2009 by
Dundee University Press
University of Dundee
Dundee DD1 4HN

www.dup.dundee.ac.uk

ISBN 978 1 84586 062 2

No natural forests were destroyed to make this product;
only farmed timber was used and replanted.

British Library Cataloguing-in-Publication Data
A catalogue record for this book is available on request from the British Library

Typeset by Waverley Typesetters, Fakenham
Printed and bound by Bell & Bain Ltd, Glasgow

CONTENTS

TABLE OF CASES

TABLE OF STATUTES

Page

1 INTRODUCTION

SCOTS COMMON LAW OF PROPERTY

The Scots common law of property is strongly realist in its concepts. In the main the common law restricts itself to tangible objects (corporeal moveable property) or to land and things attached to it. Ownership is the bundle of rights that the owner possesses. These rights can be likened to a legal wall built around the property in question and protecting it for the exclusive use of the owner. Only the owner has the right to carry out the usual juridical acts associated with property ownership (namely to sell, give away, lease/rent, license the use of the property, or offer the property as security for debt), and the owner has the right to enjoy the fruits of the property himself, or civilly through tenants or others enjoying the property with his permission. In particular, the owner has the right to prevent third parties from interfering with the property or removing it from his possession. Removal of corporeal moveable property against the owner's consent constitutes the common law crime of theft. Incorporeal property such as intellectual property rights and information rights do not fit easily with the realist attitude of Scots common law.

THE IMPOTENCE OF THE COMMON LAW CRIME OF THEFT

Things can be stolen only if they can be physically possessed and physically moved from one place to another. The common law of theft has long acknowledged that documents, deeds and certificates that evidence the existence of incorporeal rights in property may be stolen, but in these cases, what is stolen is not the incorporeal right of property itself but only the piece of paper upon which those rights depend. Intangible rights cannot be stolen and no extension has been made to this principle to cover intellectual property rights or information rights. For offences involving the misappropriation or misuse of these incorporeal rights, special statutory provision is required. Two Scots law cases stand out for particular note.

In *HM Advocate* v *Mackenzie* (1913), a husband and a wife were indicted to answer a charge of stealing a book containing chemical recipes and a second charge of making copies of certain of the recipes with the intent to sell them for profit and thereby breaching an agreement of confidence that existed between them and the owner of the recipes. It was held that only the first charge of theft of the book of recipes was relevant. In finding the second charge irrelevant, the court declined to extend the common law to cover the incorporeal rights of ownership in the recipes themselves. At this stage, we should note that an important feature of intellectual property rights is that where copies of it are taken (stolen, if you will) without the owner's consent, the original copy is usually still left in the possession of the owner. The copies may be misappropriated but their "theft" does not usually deprive the owner of his possession of the intellectual property or information concerned. Instead, the effect of such misappropriation is usually a loss of opportunity to exploit economically the rights in question. Sometimes the true owner may lose market share thereby.

In *Grant* v *Allan* (1988), the courts once again refused to extend the idea of theft to cover incorporeal intellectual property rights. In this case, an employee, in breach of a confidentiality relationship, took computer printouts of the employer's customers and their dealings, intending to supply them to a business competitor in exchange for a sum of money. The accused made a preliminary plea to the relevance of the prosecutor's complaint, stating that it was not a crime known to the law of Scotland. It was suggested by the Crown in the appeal that this was a case where the declaratory power of the High Court of Justiciary should be used to declare the conduct criminal. Such conduct, if not criminalised, would have far-reaching effects in a technological age. The court declined to use the declaratory power and stated that such an extension of the criminal law was properly a matter for legislation.

THE BREADTH OF THE UK INTELLECTUAL PROPERTY AND INFORMATION LAWS

It is therefore clear that we must rely upon statute law as our primary source of law concerning incorporeal intellectual property rights and other rights in information. Such laws are specific to the type of incorporeal right concerned and have lengthy pedigrees.

- The Copyright, Designs and Patents Act 1988, as amended, governs the protection of literary, dramatic, musical and artistic works and the indirect rights (such as film, recording and performance rights), including moral rights arising in them. This controls the economic exploitation of a very wide range of creative works.
- The Patents Act 1977 (as amended) governs the protection of registered invented products and processes.

- The Registered Designs Act 1949, together with various rules and regulations, governs registered industrial designs, while the Copyright, Designs and Patents Act 1988, as amended, governs unregistered industrial designs.

- The Trade Marks Act 1994 governs registered trade marks, names and badges of origin and quality associated with the sale of goods. A body of UK common law cases protects unregistered trade marks and names and also provides for the wrong known as passing off.

- Relationships of confidence and the protection of confidential information are also controlled by a body of UK common law cases.

In the field of information technology, there now exist provisions (the Data Protection Act 1998, for example) to protect the privacy of personal information held by third parties for lawful and business purposes. Information held by public authorities may be made available to the public under the two Freedom of Information Acts (2000 and (for Scotland) 2002). A body of other statutory provisions declares crimes certain activities relating to information and data held on computers or transmitted over computer networks. Law enforcement provision is regulated by the two Regulation of Investigatory Powers Acts (2000).

EUROPEAN AND GLOBAL MOVEMENTS

The pedigrees of many of these provisions show that they have not spontaneously evolved within the United Kingdom but are usually the product of European or even global movements made in response to industrial or technological demands. Some of these movements have produced co-operation treaties and conventions of some antiquity (such as the Paris Convention for the Protection of Industrial Property 1883, the Berne Convention of 1885 and the Madrid Agreement 1891) that have informed debate and legal provisions within Europe for a very long time. More recently, there are European Directives and Regulations which have had significant effects in shaping current United Kingdom legislation and harmonising our provisions with those of the other EU Member States. It is also important to mention the influence of the Council of Europe and its significant Conventions in harmonising human rights provisions and cybercrime provisions and co-operation both of which have strongly influenced intellectual property and information laws.

On a global level, attempts have been made by the World Trade Organization to harmonise intellectual property rights in the TRIPs

Agreement (Agreement on Trade Related Aspects of Intellectual Property 1994). The agreement has brought with it some considerable new areas of debate (for example whether it is fair to impose intellectual property provisions equally on both developed and developing countries in the latter of which perhaps questions of need override many of the provisions taken for granted in developed countries). WIPO (the World Intellectual Property Organization) has produced important treaties in the field of copyright (WIPO Copyright Treaty) and performances and phonograms (WIPO Performance and Phonograms Treaty) together sometimes referred to as the WIPO Internet Treaties.

Because these European and global movements raise such a large number of issues, it has not been possible within the scope of this volume to do them justice. Instead, we have restricted ourselves to the principal United Kingdom provisions. But the reader can expect that similar provisions will be enforceable across the European Union and in many cases (for example in the field of patents and industrial designs) the intellectual property rights owners will have to consider whether to register or re-register their rights in the relative European office. For example, it is quite possible to register a patent in the European Patent Office under a uniform application procedure seeking protection in up to 38 European countries. In addition, it is also possible to register a patent with WIPO and obtain a patent with designated states of protection.

ECONOMIC ASPECTS OF INTELLECTUAL PROPERTY RIGHTS

Despite European and global movements, the United Kingdom legislature and judiciary have tended to emphasise the economic aspects of intellectual property rights. Our European neighbours have been much more ready to recognise and protect non-economic rights such as moral rights (which appeared in UK copyright law only recently).

The ownership of monopoly rights (as occurs, for example, with patents, trade marks and registered design rights) gives the rights-holders an economic advantage in trade that can be measured economically in terms of the sales generated as a result of the product or name protected. As such, intellectual property rights are assets of business and will therefore appear on the balance sheets of businesses that own them and that therefore rely on them to generate turnover.

This raises interesting questions for accountants. Among those questions is how such intellectual property rights are to be valued when they appear on a balance sheet. Alternative approaches to this question have occurred. There are difficulties in assessing a market value for unique incorporeal assets and so some other justifications are required for valuation. Some think that the true value of the rights should be the investment that the organisation has made in obtaining these rights (either the historical cost of purchase of these rights or, where the rights have arisen inhouse, the historical costs of any internal research and development including the costs of obtaining legal protection for the rights). But it now appears that the best method is to take a "goodwill" approach where the valuation of the trend of customers to generate turnover is definitive. Where annual turnover can be ascribed to the ownership of a business of identifiable intellectual property, the turnover rate (income) can be capitalised on the basis of the accounting ROCE ratio for the business sector concerned (ROCE is the return on capital employed for the assets of that particular business sector). Broadly, if a company invests £100,000 in a bank it might expect to receive 4 per cent or 5 per cent gross interest per annum on the deposit. Where capital is worked, rather than merely invested, the ROCE is likely to be higher. Accountants use a range of such ratios (for example ROCE, RONW (return on net worth) or ROE (return on equity)) to equate the capital value of an asset with its capability to generate turnover. While such ratios are primarily intended to assess whether the business is performing appropriately, they can also provide a means for stating the future revenue-generating capacity of assets as a capital value. However, a problem with capitalisation of incorporeal assets in this way is that it requires regular review and possibly revaluation which can inflate or deflate profitability in any one reporting year. It should therefore be approached more as an estimate of the assets' economic value rather than as the value etched in stone.

2 COPYRIGHT – PART I: WHAT IS PROTECTED

Most students have some direct encounter with copyright as a form of intellectual property. They know that photocopying a book is prohibited because copyright is the legal right an individual has to prevent others from copying or reproducing their created work. They may also be aware that copyright, like other forms of intellectual property, is mainly about protecting the owner's economic interests. But they may not know what kinds of non-commercial acts they are permitted to do without breaching copyright law. And they may have only a vague idea of what kinds of property fall under the jurisdiction of copyright law as opposed to other forms of intellectual property protection. To understand copyright, we must first understand the kinds of work that are protected.

HISTORICAL BACKGROUND

The first English copyright system was created in 1556 when members of the Stationers' Company were given powers to register their printed books with the company in London. Unregistered books could be searched out and destroyed. At its inception this was a means of preventing politically and religiously dangerous works from being published, but gradually this system of registration provided publishers with a means of protecting their own registered books by preventing other persons from copying them. A form of copyright had therefore developed.

This English system did not apply to Scotland which was a wholly separate legal jurisdiction at the time and as a result it was common for books to be imported here from England and from other foreign countries and then reprinted here. The justification for the reprinting (apart from providing Scottish publishers with a source of income) was that it was considered that Scottish people should have the right to acquire knowledge and learn from reading works published in other countries. This worthy motive caused no problems in Scotland until the early part of the 18th century when Scotland and England became a United Kingdom. There was initially no restriction on English books being reprinted in Scotland and sold here. But problems began to occur when copies of these reprinted books were taken back to England. Some started asking why Scots publishers should be allowed to make money out of English authors. And so it became apparent that there should be one copyright regime for the whole United Kingdom. This was achieved by the first copyright statute – the Statute of Anne of 1710, which gave to authors a renewable copyright period of 14 years. It should be noted that this statute was highly innovative in that it placed the copyright for the first time into the hands of authors and also created a number of copyright libraries each of which was entitled to receive a copy of all UK published books. In Scotland this right was given to the Faculty of Advocates and is now vested in the National Library of Scotland.

Since 1710, the class of works which were protected by copyright has extended from printed books to include a very wide range of other materials. A large leap forward was made in the Berne Copyright Convention of 1885 which set out to codify intellectual property copyright protections across the Convention states. In the 1970s there were a number of significant reforms and, in 1988, based upon an EC Directive, the current Copyright, Designs and Patents Act came into force.

The 1988 Act as currently standing (subject to certain amendments) deals not only with copyright but also with related rights, moral rights of authors, performers' rights, and unregistered design rights (which we will come to later). And some similar but specialist rights, such as semiconductor topography rights, have become protected by subsequent EU Directives.

THE CATEGORIES OF PROTECTED WORKS

The principal categories of copyright protected works are what are known as "primary" or "authorial" works, or perhaps better as "LDMA" works. These are original:

- literary works;
- dramatic works;
- musical works; and
- artistic works.

There are also what might be called "entrepreneurial", "secondary" or "derivative" works which do not require to be original in the same sense and are:

- sound recordings;
- films;
- broadcasts; and
- typographical arrangements of published editions (the typography right in facsimile editions).

These secondary works all involve ways of further exploiting the primary works economically – so that, for example, where a musician's composition is recorded as a CD, the original musician, performers and recording producer will all have interests in protecting their continuing income streams from the published work. Commercial works, then, may involve a number of different forms of copyright interest existing concurrently. To understand these various categories of copyright work, we will first look at what the primary or LDMA works consist in. These works are defined in the early sections of the 1988 Act (ss 3 and 4).

Literary works

Literary works are published works consisting principally of words, whether written, printed, spoken, sung or otherwise displayed or recorded. The statutory definition is given in s 3(1) of the 1988 Act as:

> "any work, other than a dramatic or musical work, which is written, spoken or sung, and accordingly includes –
> (a) a table or compilation other than a database;
> (b) a computer program;
> (c) preparatory design material for a computer program; and
> (d) a database."

Thus, literary works need not be "literature" as such but would appear to include any form of original published work that consists principally of words. The question of what is included in this category was examined in *University of London Press Ltd* v *University Tutorial Press Ltd* (1916). In this case, a tutorial college, catering for school students intending to sit the University of London's external examinations in mathematics, printed copies of the university's past exam papers. It did so without the permission of the university which then claimed copyright in the questions, claiming that they were an original literary work. In its defence, the Tutorial Press argued that the ideas involved in the questions were mathematical ideas well known to most mathematicians and so the questions could not be "original works" and thus were not capable of copyright protection. The court disagreed and said that "literary works" were "works expressed in print or writing, irrespective of the question whether the quality or style is high" and in connection with originality, the courts are "not concerned with the originality of ideas, but with the expression ... of thought in print or writing". The form in which the questions appeared had to be the product of the examiners' knowledge and time spent but this need not be very substantial. By copying and printing the exam papers, infringement had indeed taken place.

From this case and other similar cases we can take three important points. First, we see that the work is not literature in the sense that we might use that word to describe a classic novel; rather, a "literary work" simply implies words or other similar features written or printed or otherwise reproduced (in an original fixed form). Second, we see that it is not the underlying ideas themselves but the original expression of those ideas which are protected. And third, for words to be protected as literary work, they must at least demonstrate the creator's skill, labour and judgement, and in particular the work must have some merit, or impart some instruction, information or pleasure. It follows from this analysis that single words or the titles of films are not protectable by copyright unless they are of sufficient length, inventiveness, entertainment or instruction as to indicate creative merit.

To underline these conclusions, the issue in *Ladbroke (Football) Ltd* v *William Hill (Football) Ltd* (1964) involved a football pools coupon which the court held could be regarded as a protectable original literary work in the sense that it involved some skill and labour in the design and layout.

As a result of the statutory wording and of these cases, we can see that literary works include all books, magazines, newspapers, published articles, poems and so on, whether in fact, written, printed, spoken, sung or displayed electronically (say, over the Internet). All that is required is that these works, involving principally words, should be published or reproduced in a fixed form.

In recent times it was not clear whether this definition included printed electronic circuit diagrams or whether those should better be regarded as artistic works. In fact, a recent case held that there was no reason why literary and artistic copyrights could not reside in the same work. Computer chip printed circuit diagrams and the silicon chips made from them are now protected separately by Pt 3 of the 1988 Act, as amended by the Design Right (Semiconductor Topographies) Regulations 1989.

Dramatic works

The 1988 Act defines dramatic works as including "a work of dance or mime" (s 3(1)). This skeletal definition has had to be given content by case law and has some odd consequences. For example, the performance of a song by someone dressed in costume would not be a dramatic work but by virtue of the statutory definitions would be a literary or, alternatively, a musical work. So, how have the courts interpreted "dramatic"? They have tended to interpret dramatic works as being works of action capable of public performance.

Even this has proved problematic. In the case of *Norowzian* v *Arks Ltd (No 2)* (2000), an advertisement film producer used a technique of editing and composing film frames (called "jump cutting") that enabled a person to be shown acting in a physically impossible manner. The resultant film (*Anticipation*) showed a man apparently dancing in a quirky jerky fashion while waiting for a pint of Guinness to settle. The plaintiff claimed that this breached the copyright in a film called *Joy* that he had made in 1992 using the same jump-cutting technique. In the court of first instance, the English High Court, it was held that the film was not a dramatic work since the appearance of dancing was the product of a film editing technique only and was incapable of being actually performed by an individual on a public stage. However, the Court of Appeal held that a dramatic work could include a film made by jump cutting because the film could itself be performed publicly before an audience. The film *Joy* was not a recording of a dramatic work of action since the work could not be physically performed, however, the film itself could be considered as a dramatic work because it depicted movement and was "a work of action with or without words or music which is capable of being performed before an audience". However, it was decided that though both *Joy* and *Anticipation* were dramatic works created using the same editing technique, this was not enough to establish infringement of copyright. The court held that as no individual frame of the film *Joy* had been copied in the Guinness advert, there had been no copying of the expression of the ideas and so no copyright infringement.

Musical works

"Music" is not defined in the 1988 Act (s 3(1) merely says that "'musical work' means a work consisting of music, exclusive of any words or action intended to be sung, spoken or performed with the music") and so we must use a dictionary definition to understand what the term means. A useful such definition of "music" may be "the art of combining vocal and/or instrumental sounds in a harmonious and expressive way; the printed or written score of this; a pleasant natural sound".

Recently, Mike Batt, who promoted both the Wombles and Vanessa Mae, released an album (*Classical Grafitti*) that contained a 60-second silent track. He was surprised to receive a claim of copyright infringement from the representatives of the avant-garde composer John Cage, who died in 1992 and who had created a famous silent work called *4'33"*

(4 minutes 33 seconds) that consisted of a silence of that length, recorded live. Rather than test the claim in court, Mike Batt is believed to have paid an undisclosed six-figure sum to John Cage's representatives. This indicates that it may be possible to have musical copyright in silence!

In another case, *Lawson* v *Dundas* (1985), it was held that Channel 4's original signature tune was a protected musical work even though in fact its principal idea consisted of only four notes.

So it seems that "musical work" involves any work whereby sounds are published or notated in a fixed form. This would include both musical scores and the distinctive music that is performed from them. These cover the main forms of musical works as planned by composers. We shall see later that authorised recordings of musical works give rise to secondary rights known as recording rights and there are also performers' rights which authorised performers may have in their own performances.

Derivative works

Readers should notice that the original copyright owner also has rights in derivative works such as transcriptions, arrangements and translations of the original work. This clearly particularly applies to musical works where it is common to rearrange an existing work for performance by special instruments or performers or for special occasions where only parts of a work can be performed, but derivative works are also very important in connection with literary works where, for example, an author has right in translations of their work.

Artistic works

The 1988 Act defines these very widely (in s 4) and says that these include graphic works (drawings, paintings, diagrams, maps, charts, engravings or similar), photographs, sculptures or collages (all the foregoing being irrespective of artistic quality) and also works of architecture (being buildings or parts of a building or models for a building) and works of artistic craftsmanship. Just as for literary works, readers should notice that the first group of artistic works are protected irrespective of artistic quality. Works of architecture and artistic craftsmanship do require artistic quality. This has given rise to a number of cases, particularly as to where and how mass-produced items containing design elements can be protected under copyright.

In *Wham-O Manufacturing* v *Lincoln* (1985), the issue concerned whether the preliminary drawings, wooden prototype models, metal moulds and finished plastic "Frisbee" products could be protected under copyright. The court held that since the aim of artistic copyright was to protect original artistic works, it followed that the drawings were protected as graphic works, the wooden models and the metal moulds were both protected as sculptures, but the finished plastic "Frisbees" were not protected under copyright. Chief Justice Davison said: "it seems inappropriate to regard utilitarian objects such as plastic flying discs, manufactured as toys, by an injection moulding process, as items of sculpture for the purposes of the Copyright Act. They lack any expressive form of the creator and any idea which the creator seeks to convey". In *Metix UK Ltd* v *G H Maughan (Plastics) Ltd* (1997), the Patents Court affirmed that a mould for making a functional article was not protected as a work of sculpture for copyright purposes.

Given that there is a tendency away from protecting mass-produced, commercial or utilitarian articles as types of artistic work under copyright, there have been a number of cases where manufacturers have attempted to protect their commercial designs as forms of artistic craftsmanship because this category appears subjectively to cover a wider range of situations.

In *Merlet* v *Mothercare* (1986), a baby's "Raincosy" cape and hood were regarded as an article serving a primarily functional purpose whereas craftsmanship and design and other aesthetic concerns were regarded as purely secondary matters. Walton J said: "when creating the 'Raincosy' Mme Merlet did not have in mind the creation of a work of art in any shape or form. What she had in mind, as appeared quite clearly from her evidence, was the utilitarian consideration of creating a barrier between the assumed rigours of a Highland summer and her baby in such a manner as would afford him complete protection".

In *Guild* v *Eskandaar Ltd* (2001), a peasant-style shirt, sweater and dress were held not to be protected by copyright as there was no evidence before the court that the designer intended to create works of art or that she regarded herself as an artist. The works had been created for commercial production.

There have also been other cases where what can be copyrightable has been questioned. In *Kenrick Co* v *Lawrence & Co* (1890), a pointing hand design made from a simple graphic drawing into a typeface was held to be a copyright work and has been used by printers ever since. The court held that infringement would occur only when a virtually identical design was used (copying the expression of the underlying idea) but there was no reason why a person should not make their own drawing of a hand and use it in a similar way (copying merely the idea).

In *Antiquesportfolio.com plc* v *Rodney Fitch* (2001), the court held that the photographer of a photographic work manifested artistic craftsmanship in his choice of subject-matter, lighting, positioning and camera angle.

Sound recordings

In the field of secondary works, where the protection of commercial interests is the primary concern, a sound recording is defined in the 1988 Act as "a recording of sounds, from which the sounds may be reproduced, or a recording of the whole or any part of a literary, dramatic or musical work, from which sounds reproducing the work or part maybe reproduced" (s 5A(1)(a) and (b)). The statute goes on to say that these are protected regardless of the medium in which the recording has been made. With sound recordings there is no originality requirement. The soundtrack attached to a film is now regarded as part of the film (s 5B(2)).

Films and broadcasts

A "film" is defined as "a recording in any medium from which a moving image may be, by any means, reproduced" (s 5B(1)). This definition therefore includes DVDs, video tapes, and movies and also stills from these. Film rights also extend to the sound rights recorded with a film.

"Broadcasts" are defined as a non-interactive electronic transmission of visual images, sounds or information transmitted for simultaneous public reception or at a time determined solely by the broadcaster (Copyright and Related Rights Regulations 2003). This definition includes Internet live web casts and simulcasts and also web casts scheduled at times determined by the broadcaster. But other Internet transmissions are not protected as broadcasts but are likely to be separately protected as LDMA works.

In the cases of both film and broadcasts, the copyrights concerned are derivative rights resting in the producers of the film or broadcast. It should be noted that the author also has rights in films and broadcasts and can prevent further copying so that the film and broadcast rights can derive only from authorised productions.

Typographic arrangements

These rights protect facsimiles of existing typographic arrangements. "Facsimile" means an exact copy of the original page layouts.

In *Newspaper Licensing* v *Marks & Spencer* (2003), the store collated and reproduced certain newspaper cuttings taken from a press agency. It was held that this was not an infringement of typography rights because such an infringement would require the exact reproduction of the page concerned. The court held that "nothing short of a facsimile copy would suffice".

Adaptations

As we have seen, adaptations are also protected and these relate to literary, dramatic and musical works. An adaptation of a literary and dramatic work can include a translation, a conversion of a dramatic work into a non-dramatic format and vice versa, the reproduction of a work in the form of the story conveyed by pictures for inclusion in a book, a musical or a magazine, and so on.

In relation to musical works, "adaptation" means an arrangement or transcription.

In relation to computer programs, "adaptation" means the conversion of the program from one computer language to another.

PERFORMERS' RIGHTS

A performer in public, providing that he is authorised by the owner of the original work to perform the work in question, has the right to say who and for what purposes their performance may be recorded (s 182 *et seq* of the 1988 Act). This is sometimes referred to as the performer's property rights in their performances and in recordings of their performances. These property rights are:

- *reproduction right*: the right to copy the recording;
- *distribution right*: the right to issue recordings to the public; and
- *rental and lending right*: the right to rent or lend a recording to the public.

It can be seen that these are rights to economic remuneration derived from the performance.

Recordings requiring consent cover a wide range of performances, including dramatic and musical performances; readings and recitations of literary works; and variety, circus and comedy acts. Recording rights in a performance can be given only by the performer and so commercial recording rights are usually embodied in exclusive recording contracts between the performer and the recording producer.

Copying, lending or renting existing recordings are also controlled but there is an exemption for the copying of a recording made for purely private and domestic uses (s 182A(1)).

A performer has "non-property" rights in their performance, meaning that he has additional rights to take action against any person who unlawfully records or broadcasts a performance without consent. The performer's non-property rights are also infringed when an illicit recording is shown or broadcast without consent, or is knowingly imported for commercial purposes without consent.

MORAL RIGHTS

In addition to copyright protections, which are economic rights, there are also the moral rights of the author or creator. The Performances (Moral Rights) Regulations 2006 now extend these rights to performers.

There are three types of moral rights:

1. the "*paternity right*", being the right of the author or performer to be identified as such;
2. the "*integrity right*", being the right of the author or performer to object to derogatory treatment of the work (a deletion, alteration, or adaptation that distorts or mutilates the work or would be prejudicial to the honour and reputation of the author or performer would breach this integrity right);
3. the right of an author or creator of a work not to have the work *falsely attributed*.

These are not economic rights but integrity right can have certain economic consequences. Moral rights require to be asserted and cannot be assigned.

ARTIST'S RESALE RIGHT

An artist (of graphics, pictures, paintings, photographs and sculptures) has certain rights to a royalty on the commercial resale of an original work (but only where the work is sold for 1,000 euros or more). This right does not arise where the sale is between two private individuals.

DATABASE RIGHTS

While databases are protected by the 1988 Act as literary works comprising compilations of data, a database right is also provided for by the Copyright and Designs in Databases Regulations 1997, as amended by the Copyright and Rights in Databases (Amendment) Regulations 2003 which protect any database and its contents where there has been "a substantial investment in obtaining, verifying and presenting the contents of the database" (reg 13 of the 1997 Regulations). In this way not only is it prohibited to copy databases but it is also unlawful to extract and reuse data taken from a protected database.

HOW LONG DO THE PROTECTIONS LAST?

Copyright in most cases lasts for 70 years from the end of the year in which the author or creator dies. Copyright in computer-generated works lasts for 50 years from the end of the year in which they were made. Copyright in sound recordings last for 50 years from the end of the year in which they were made or released. Copyright in a film lasts for 50 years from the end of the year in which the last of the principal director, author of the screenplay or dialogue, or composer of the music dies. Copyright in typographical arrangements lasts for 25 years from the end of the year in which the arrangement was published. Copyright in artistic works which have been industrially exploited lasts for 25 years (s 52 of the 1988 Act). Moral rights last as long as the copyrights last, except for false attribution right which lasts for 20 years from the end of the year in which the author dies. Database rights last for 15 years from the end of the year in which the database was first made available.

Essential Facts

- Copyright is the right that an author has to prevent their work from being reproduced – usually to the economic detriment of the author.
- Protected works involve the author's expression of his ideas in a fixed form. The ideas themselves are not protected.
- The principal categories of work that are protected are original literary, dramatic, musical and artistic works. These are often referred to as "primary" or "authorial" works. "Secondary" or

"derivative" works are also protected. These are sound recordings, films (including their soundtracks), broadcasts and typographical arrangements.

- Literary works are works consisting of words (whether written, printed, spoken or sung). The works must be of sufficient length to indicate some merit, inventiveness, entertainment or instruction. A literary work also includes a table, compilation, computer program or database.

- A dramatic work is a work of action and including dance and mime but excluding words (which are covered by literary works protections).

- Musical works involve sounds (usually instrumental) whose form is controlled by the instructions of the composer (but again excluding words).

- Artistic works includes a very broad range of creative materials (including graphic works, photographs, sculptures, collages, works of architecture and works of artistic craftsmanship). The first four of these categories are protected regardless of artistic quality. The last two require artistic quality to be demonstrated.

- Works which have artistic quality as a secondary objective (for example, mass-produced items, commercial items, and items not intended by the creators principally as works of art) are less likely to be granted copyright protection as artistic works.

- Soundtracks are recordings of sounds (of any nature) from which the sounds may be reproduced. These are perhaps most important commercially in the area of musical recordings.

- Films include recordings in any medium of a moving image (and also include the soundtracks associated with films).

- Broadcasts are non-interactive transmissions of visual images, sounds and other information transmitted for simultaneous reception by viewers or for reception at a time determined solely by the broadcaster.

- Typographic arrangements are facsimile copies of original published layouts.

- Adaptations of the primary or authorial works are also protected.

- Performers have rights in their performances and can say who and for what purpose their performances are recorded. They also have rights in the distribution, rental and lending of recordings of their performances.

- Copyright law also includes moral rights of authors and performers. These non-economic rights involve: the right of the author or performer to be identified as such; rights against derogatory treatment of their work; and rights of an author or creator against false attribution.

- Additional database protections exist under regulations.

Essential Cases

University of London Press Ltd v University Tutorial Press Ltd (1916): a tutorial college printed copies of the University of London's past exam papers, without permission. The court held that form in which the questions appeared was protected since it was the product of the examiners' knowledge and time spent devising the questions.

Ladbroke (Football) Ltd v William Hill (Football) Ltd (1964): the court held that a football pools coupon could be regarded as a protectable original literary work in the sense that it involved some skill and labour in the design and layout.

Norowzian v Arks Ltd (No 2) (2000): an advertisement film producer used a technique of editing and composing film frames called "jump cutting" that enabled a dancer to be shown moving jerkily in a manner that was physically impossible. The plaintiff claimed dramatic copyright in the editing technique which he had previously used in his film *Joy*. The Court of Appeal held that a dramatic work could include a film made by jump cutting because the film depicted dance (a work of action) and the film could be performed publicly before an audience. However, the film *Joy* was not infringed since no individual frame of the film had been copied in the later advert. The jump-cutting technique was not protected under copyright.

Lawson v Dundas (1985): it was held that Channel 4's original signature tune was a protected musical work even though in fact its principal idea consisted of only four notes. The notes in combination were, however, very distinctive.

Wham-O Manufacturing v Lincoln (1985): design drawings for plastic toy "Frisbees" were protected as graphic works, wooden models and the metal moulds for them were protected as sculptures but the finished plastic "Frisbees" were not protected under copyright.

Metix UK Ltd v G H Maughan (Plastics) Ltd (1997): a mould for making a functional article was not protected as a work of sculpture for copyright purposes.

Merlet v Mothercare (1986): a baby's "Raincosy" cape and hood were regarded as an article serving a primarily functional purpose where craftsmanship and design and other aesthetic concerns were regarded as purely secondary matters.

Guild v Eskandaar Ltd (2001): a peasant-style shirt, sweater and dress were held not to be protected by copyright. The designer had not intended to create works of art nor did she regard herself as an artist. The works had been created for commercial production.

Antiquesportfolio.com plc v Rodney Fitch (2001): a photographic work showed artistic craftsmanship in the choice of subject-matter, lighting, positioning and camera angle.

Newspaper Licensing v Marks & Spencer (2003): it was not an infringement of typography rights to copy newspaper articles cut and pasted from a news service. The court held that "nothing short of a facsimile copy would suffice".

3 COPYRIGHT – PART II: OTHER ISSUES

While the types of intellectual property protected by copyright were outlined in Chapter 2, this chapter continues our examination of copyright by examining the nature of copyright ownership, licences, and the infringing acts which copyright sets out to prohibit. The chapter closes with a consideration of various other matters with which copyright law is concerned.

OWNERSHIP OF COPYRIGHT

Copyright is statutorily defined as a property right (Copyright, Designs and Patents Act 1988, s 1(1)). Section 9 of the Act states that the author of a copyright work is the person who creates that work and goes on to define who the "author" is in relation to each type of primary and secondary work. Section 11 states that the author of the work is the first owner. However, there are two situations in which this is not the case.

Section 11(2) provides that "where a literary, dramatic, musical or artistic work, or a film, is made by an employee in the course of his employment, his employer is the first owner of any copyright in the work subject to any agreement to the contrary". Whether an employee is employed to be creative is an issue which will be examined further in Chapter 5 when we examine patents, for there are a number of important cases. However, it is usual to look first at the contract of employment; thereafter to look to whether the employer has provided resources for the purposes of creativity; and lastly to whether the employee spent working time upon the creative tasks. It is generally held that where an employer has set aside resources for the purposes of an employee's creativity, then the first ownership passes to the employer. One way of looking at this is that, but for the employment relationship, the employee would not be making creative work at all.

Another associated issue arises in connection with commissions. Here the "but for" test is not so clear. Under the Copyright Act 1956, the commissioner owned the copyright since, but for the commission, the work would not exist. But under the 1988 Act, commissioners do not own the copyright in the created work. Instead commissioners obtain some rights of use of the material. Other rights remain vested in the author. The general view of the courts is that while commissioners have rights to use the created material, all other rights remain with the author unless the commissioner is able to establish that they had a material degree of control over the form of the created work. This view is demonstrated in the case of *Beckingham* v *Hodgens* (2003) where it was established that any person must show a "significant and original contribution to the creation of the work" before they may be regarded as a joint owner, a contribution which "approximated to penmanship ... a direct responsibility for what actually appeared on the page". For those reasons, the employment of a specialist photographer to record a social event will leave the photographer holding the copyright in the photographs, while the commissioner will have reasonable rights to use the photographs for normal private and domestic purposes. This could raise issues regarding the further use which a photographer might have in photographs. This is dealt with in s 85 of the 1988 Act, which states that a person who commissions a photographer to record private and domestic photographs or films is entitled to a right not to have copies of the works issued to the public, exhibited or shown in public, or broadcast.

LICENCES

Apart from the above restrictions, the owner of the copyright is entitled to normal juridical rights concerning their property in the created work. This means that they have the right to sell or give away their rights in the created work or to loan or mortgage the same. In addition, they may wish to exploit their rights by means of licences. There are no restrictions on the kind of rights which can be exercised through a licence nor are there restrictions on the formal requirements for a licence. However, especially where licences relate to substantial economic exploitations of copyright, they will usually be granted in writing. Occasionally licences are given orally or by implication. But in these cases there are serious problems for both licensor and licensee in proving the terms of implied or oral licences.

In the case of *Film Investors Overseas Services SA* v *Home Video Channel Ltd* (1997) plaintiffs were held to have consented to or acquiesced in the infringing activity which they either knew or strongly expected to have been taking place for some years.

Licences, and particularly exclusive licences, are a most important way in which a copyright owner can exploit their creation. In this way an owner may allow one party to exercise all the owner's rights within a legal jurisdiction in exchange for a royalty. The exclusive licensee stands, as it were, in the shoes of the owner within that jurisdiction and is entitled to sue infringers for damages that may be, but for the licence agreement, due to the owner. An exclusive licensee is therefore in a very powerful position.

Implied licences, on the other hand, can be very weak and it is often a problem to establish what are their exact terms, duration and extent, what it is that is permitted, what royalty payments are due, and in what circumstances the licence will come to an end.

INFRINGEMENT – THE RESTRICTED ACTS

The principal acts prohibited by copyright law have an economic character and are all acts which either prevent the copyright owner from deriving economic value from their rights, or alternatively, enable the infringer to take an unfair profit at the copyright owner's expense. These infringing acts are summarised in ss 17–21 of the 1988 Act. They are primary infringements. (For secondary infringements, see below.) The primary infringing acts are:

- Section 17: Copying the work in any material form, though what counts as copying varies from situation to situation. In some cases, copying may be literally from one original form into another similar form: for example, making a photocopy of a literary work. It is equally not permissible to copy a work into another form: for example, to scan a literary work into a digital format for retention and subsequent viewing on a computer screen. Nor is it permissible to reproduce a two-dimensional work in a three-dimensional form or vice versa.

- Section 18: Issuing copies to the public. "Distribution right" requires payment of a royalty to enable the owner to profit from circulation of copies. But additional royalties are payable for extended distribution where, for example, lending or rental rights are involved.

- Section 19: Performing, showing or playing a literary, dramatic or musical work in public (but not the public exhibition of artistic works), which requires payment of royalties for any visual or acoustic rendition. A performer's rights are also infringed if a recorded performance is shown to the public without consent.

- Section 20: The unauthorised broadcasting of a literary, dramatic, musical or artistic work, sound recording, film or broadcast.

- Section 21: The unauthorised adaptation (translation, transcription, arrangement or alteration) of a literary, dramatic or musical work; s 21 also prohibits certain other acts done in pursuance of adaptations.

SUBSTANTIALITY

For any infringement to be upheld, it is essential that it should be shown that there has been copying or another restricted act of "the whole or a substantial part" of the protected work (s 16(3)(a)).

The question of what constitutes a substantial part was considered in the case of *Designers Guild Ltd* v *Russell Williams (Textiles) Ltd* (2000). This case involved copyright in a fabric which contained stripes of flowers and leaves placed in an "impressionistic" manner. The plaintiffs alleged that the defendants' similar fabric infringed their own. The court carried out a visual comparison between the two fabrics and formulated a four-point test for infringement. The court decided that:

- substantiality was measured qualitatively and not quantitatively (it is not the percentage of the total that is used to measure substantiality but rather the contribution that the part copied makes to the whole work);
- the opposite of substantial is insignificant;
- in determining substantiality no weight is to be given to anything that is commonplace, well known, or derived from another source (ie not original); and
- the object of copyright law is to protect primarily the product of an author's skill and labour. Copyright is not there to create an economic monopoly in the ideas underlying a work.

PARALLEL IMPORTS AND EXHAUSTION OF RIGHTS

Parallel imports occur where articles are imported when this is in contravention of copyright rights or exclusive licences. It is clear that if copies of a music CD were subject to an exclusive licence in the UK and illegal copies were produced in the Far East and subsequently imported for commercial purposes into the UK without payment of royalties, then such copies would be illegal. No royalties would have been paid for these copies and the exclusive licensee in the UK would be able to take action against the importer to recover damages. A similar situation occurs where there are exclusive licences to conduct certain acts in one jurisdiction but products are thereafter subject to parallel importation into the UK to take advantage of the difference in royalty fees. It is quite likely that the costs of royalties in the Far East would be considerably less than the cost of the same royalties if issued in the UK. It may therefore be a financially viable proposition for a parallel importer to pay lower royalty fees in one part of the world and then import into another and exploit the difference. For example, if there existed an inexpensive licence in Malaysia to produce copies of a music CD for sale only in Malaysia and copies of those CDs were imported into the UK in order to profit from the fact that fees in the UK were higher, the situation in that case would also be one of parallel importation and an exclusive licensee in the UK is again entitled to take action against the parallel importer to prevent this economic abuse.

A similar but different situation occurs as a consequence of the European Single Market as there is a standing principle of European law which allows the free movement of goods and services within the European Economic Area. However, in this case there is a competition between the concept of parallel importation and the concept of a single market. Such a situation occurred in the case of *Warner Bros Inc* v *Christiansen* (1988) where the plaintiffs had licensed a Danish licensee to distribute and rent copies of a film there. At the time no licence to rent copies had been granted in the UK. Christiansen bought copies of the film in the UK and imported them into Denmark where he rented them. It was held by the court that the Danish licensee had the right to demand royalties from Christiansen for the rental of the film there. However, where royalties have been paid in one EU country and the work is imported and issued to the public in another EU country in a form for which royalties have been paid in the first country, then no additional royalties are payable since the owner (or their representative) is deemed already to have been paid. This principle is referred to as "exhaustion of rights".

Another consequence of the EU is that exclusive licences may not be used to create conditions of unfair competition. This would be contrary to Arts 81 and 82 of the Treaty of Rome. In the case of *Volvo AB* v *Erik Veng UK Ltd* (1988) Volvo had refused to license the production of spare parts in the UK but it was held that there was no evidence of abuse of a dominant position unless there was evidence of overpricing or refusing to supply spare parts to non-franchised dealers.

SECONDARY INFRINGEMENT AND COPY-PROTECTION DEVICES

Secondary infringement is governed by ss 22–26 of the 1988 Act and concerns commercial dealings with items (most of which will be the products of primary infringement). The sections define the secondary infringing acts as follows:

- Section 22 prohibits the importing of an infringing copy of a work.
- Section 23 prohibits possession or commercial dealing in infringing copies.
- Section 24 states that it is a secondary infringement of copyright to provide various sorts of means intended for the making of infringing copies.
- Sections 25 and 26 state that it is a secondary infringement to permit premises to be used for the giving of an infringing performance of a literary, dramatic or musical work or to provide apparatus for giving an infringing performance.

In each case, it is essential to show that the secondary infringer had the requisite element of knowledge: usually meaning that they knew or had reason to believe that the acts concerned involved dealing in an infringing copy or involvement in an infringing performance.

The principles of secondary infringement are carried across to include copy protection devices. Section 296 of the 1988 Act prevents the importation, sale, hire, or advertising of a device which is designed or adapted to get around legitimate copy-protection devices.

STATUTORY FAIR DEALING EXEMPTIONS – THE "PERMITTED ACTS"

Copyright involves achieving a fair balance between conflicting rights (which include balancing the legitimate right of individuals to acquire knowledge against the right of an owner to exploit their creation economically), so there exist a number permitted acts which allow a fair use of protected works. These are given in ss 28–50D of the 1988 Act.

The best known of these fair uses are as follows:

- Section 29: the right to make copies of works for the purposes of research and private study (but only where such copying is done for non-commercial purposes, is associated with a sufficient acknowledgement and is not done so as to prevent the copyright owner from making a sale or otherwise deriving a reasonable financial benefit from the work).
- Section 30: the right to copy for the purposes of criticism, review or news reporting (provided that the use is a fair dealing, that the work has been already made available to the public and there is sufficient acknowledgement). Photographs may not be used without the express permission of the copyright owner.

- Section 31: incidental inclusion of copyright material in an artistic work, sound recording, film or broadcast. In the case *IPC Magazines* v *MGN Ltd* (1998) a TV advert for the *Sunday Mirror* Sunday supplement used the front page of the plaintiffs' magazine *Woman* as the mock-up of the supplement. MGN claimed that the inclusion was incidental. The judge held that "incidental" meant casual, inessential, subordinate or background and that the inclusion in this case was not incidental as it was an essential part of the advertisement.

- Sections 32–36 provide for certain educational fair uses, being copying for instruction or examination, making anthologies, playing, showing or performing a work in an educational establishment, certain recordings and reprographic copying for the purposes of education. In each case the use must be non-commercial and a sufficient acknowledgement must be given. Performances to the public are not covered and still require a licence.

- Sections 37–44A allow certain acts of copying for library and archive purposes.

- Sections 45–50 allow copying for public administration purposes (for example, s 45 allows copies to be made for the purposes of use in judicial proceedings).

- Sections 28A and 50A–50D allow transient and other copies for the operational use of computers and databases.

The permitted acts are all non-economic uses of copyright material and they extend only so far as they do not impinge upon the economic rights of authors. For example, you can photocopy a few articles in a book, but substantial photocopying, such as would be likely to prevent the author from obtaining a sale of the book, would not be permitted.

DEFENCES

It follows from the above provision that there are a number of ways in which copyright claims can be defended:

(1) It may be possible to challenge the existence of the copyright.

(2) It may be possible to challenge the ownership of the copyright.

(3) It may be possible to deny there has been infringement.

(4) It may be possible to claim an entitlement to do the acts complained of (as a result of a formal or informal licence or permission, or because there is a public interest in doing the act concerned, or because there is a statutory fair dealing exception).

REMEDIES

The remedies open to the successful owner of copyright works include:

(1) Injunction (interdict in Scotland) (including interim injunction or interdict) – an order of the court to prevent the infringer from repeating the infringing acts complained of.

(2) Declarator – the decree of the court in which it finds and declares the ownership of the copyright and states whether there has been infringement.

(3) Damages – whereby the copyright owner can obtain compensation for loss of opportunity to exploit the work commercially. This is usually related to loss of sales or loss of royalties. A court may find that a reasonable assessment of damages would be the reasonable amount of royalties which would have been payable by the infringer if they had sought and obtained a grant of a licence for the acts complained of.

(4) Accounting for profits – where the court requires the infringer to produce evidence of any profit which he or she has made from the infringements and uses this as the basis for the estimation of damages.

(5) A court order for delivery and destruction of infringing copies.

(6) Power to prompt Trading Standards to raise criminal proceedings against the infringer. (Most of the civil rights open to copyright owners against infringers will also have associated criminal offences.)

In addition to the above there are criminal offences for communicating a copyright work. The criminal law aspects of copyright are pursued, investigated and prosecuted by the Trading Standards authorities.

Essential Facts

- **Ownership of copyright**: the author of the work is usually the first owner.
- **Ownership by employers**: where a literary, dramatic, musical or artistic work, or a film, is made by an employee in the course of his employment, the employer is the first owner subject to any agreement

to the contrary. It is generally held that where an employer has set aside resources for the purposes of employee's creativity, then the first ownership passes to the employer.

- **Commissions**: commissioners do not usually own the copyright in the created work but obtain some rights of use of the material. Other rights remain vested in the author. The commissioner may be able to establish greater rights where they show that they had a material degree of control over the form of the created work. By s 85 of the 1988 Act, a person who commissions a photographer to record private and domestic photographs or films is entitled to a right not to have copies of the works issued to the public, exhibited or shown in public, or broadcast.

- **Licences**: the owner of the copyright is entitled to normal juridical rights concerning their property in the created work. This means that they have the right to sell or give away their rights in the created work or to loan or mortgage the same. In addition, they may wish to exploit their rights by means of licences. There are no restrictions on the kind of rights which can be exercised through a licence, nor are there restrictions on the formal requirements for a licence.

- **Primary infringement**: the principal acts prohibited by copyright law have an economic character and are all acts which either prevent the copyright owner from deriving economic value from their rights, or, alternatively, enable the infringer to take an unfair profit at the copyright owner's expense. These infringing acts are summarised in ss 17–21 of the 1988 Act and include:
  - copying the work in any material form
  - issuing copies to the public
  - performing, showing or playing a literary, dramatic or musical work in public (a performer's rights are also infringed if a recorded performance is shown to the public without consent)
  - unauthorised broadcasting
  - unauthorised adaptation (translation, transcription, arrangement or alteration).

- **Substantiality of infringement**: for any infringement to be upheld, it is essential that it should be shown that there has been copying or another restricted act of "the whole or a substantial part" of the protected work (s 16(3)(a)).

- **Parallel imports**: these occur where articles are imported when this is in contravention of copyright rights or exclusive licences. A similar situation occurs where there are exclusive licences to conduct certain acts in one jurisdiction but products are thereafter subject to parallel importation into the UK to take advantage of the difference in royalty fees. The copyright owner or an exclusive licensee in the UK is entitled to take action against a parallel importer to prevent this form of economic abuse.

- **Exhaustion of rights**: as a consequence of the principle of European law which allows the free movement of goods and services within the European Economic Area, where royalties have been paid in one EU country and the work is imported and issued to the public in another EU country, no additional royalties are payable since the owner (or their representative) is deemed already to have been paid what is due to them.

- **Secondary infringement**: this involves commercial dealings with infringing copies. These are covered by ss 22–26 of the 1988 Act and prohibit importing, possession and dealing in an infringing copy, providing various sorts of means for the making of infringing copies, giving permission for premises to be used for an infringing performance, and making apparatus available for the giving of an infringing performance.

- **Statutory fair dealing exemptions:** these are permitted acts, non-economic uses of copyright material, which extend only so far as they do not impinge upon the economic rights of authors. These allow some copying for research and private study, criticism, review or news reporting, incidental inclusion of copyright material in other works, certain educational uses, some acts of copying for library, archive purposes and public administration purposes, and some transient copying for computer and database functions.

- The **remedies** open to the successful owner of copyright works include: (1) injunction (interdict); (2) declarator; (3) damages for loss suffered by the copyright owner; (4) accounting for profits made by the infringer; (5) order for delivery and destruction of infringing copies; and (6) power to prompt Trading Standards to raise criminal proceedings.

Essential Cases

Film Investors Overseas Services SA v Home Video Channel Ltd (1997): the plaintiffs were held to have consented to or acquiesced in the infringing activity which they either knew or strongly expected to have been taking place for some years.

Beckingham v Hodgens (2003): in this case concerning a commissioner of a work it was established that any person must show a "significant and original contribution to the creation of the work" before they may be regarded as a joint owner, a contribution which "approximated to penmanship ... a direct responsibility for what actually appeared on the page".

Designers Guild Ltd v Russell Williams (Textiles) Ltd (2000): this case involved copyright in a fabric which contained stripes of flowers and leaves placed in an "impressionistic" manner. The plaintiffs alleged that the defendants' similar fabric infringed their own. The court carried out a visual comparison between the two fabrics and formulated a four-point test for infringement. The court decided that: (1) substantiality was measured qualitatively and not quantitatively; (2) the opposite of substantial is insignificant; (3) anything that is commonplace, well known, or derived from another source is ignored; and (4) the object of copyright law is to protect primarily the product of an author's skill and labour and not to create an economic monopoly in the ideas underlying a work.

Warner Bros Inc v Christiansen (1988): the plaintiffs had licensed a Danish licensee to distribute and rent copies of a film there. At the time no licence to rent copies had been granted in the UK. Christiansen bought copies of the film in the UK and imported them into Denmark where he rented them. The UK price Christiansen had paid included no element for royalties for renting out the copies. It was therefore held by the court that the Danish licensee had the right to demand royalties from Christiansen for the rental of the film there.

Volvo AB v Erik Veng UK Ltd (1988): Volvo had refused to license the production of spare parts in the UK but it was held that there was no evidence of abuse of a dominant position unless there was evidence of overpricing or refusing to supply spare parts to non-franchised dealers.

IPC Magazines v MGN Ltd (1998): a TV advert for the *Sunday Mirror* Sunday supplement used the front page of the plaintiffs' magazine *Woman* as the mock- up of the supplement. MGN claimed that the inclusion was incidental. The judge held that "incidental" meant casual, inessential, subordinate or background and that the inclusion in this case was not incidental as it was an essential part of the advertisement.

4 DESIGNS

We saw in Chapter 2 that there are limitations on what can be protected under copyright law as artistic works. Industrially mass-produced items of a predominantly commercial or functional type are not classified as "artistic works" and the courts have been reluctant to extend copyright law to include such items. Design drawings for these items are regarded as graphic works and models and moulds can be protected as artistic works. One might therefore expect that reproducing a graphic work from its two-dimensional form into a three-dimensional form would be a prohibited act under copyright law but s 51 of the Copyright, Designs and Patents Act 1988 provides that it is not an infringement of copyright for an article to be made from a design document or model where that item is not an artistic work or a typeface. Only the making of artistic works (as such) and typefaces are protected. Industrially mass-produced commercial and functional items are not.

At the same time, there is clearly a need for industrially mass-produced items with a commercial value and functional purpose to be protected in order to create a market for such items with identifiable brands. There are a number of ways in which this can be achieved. In this chapter we will look at UK registered designs (which protect industrially produced items and their packaging where these have a distinctive look and feel); UK unregistered design rights (which protect primarily functional aspects of industrial products); and semiconductor topography rights (which protect the architecture of computer chips used in a range of products). For both registered designs and unregistered design rights there are European counterparts which vary slightly but depend on much the same principles.

REGISTERED DESIGNS

UK registered designs are protected under the Registered Designs Act 1949, as amended by the Copyright, Designs and Patents Act 1988 and the Registered Design Regulations 2001 and 2003.

Section 1(2) of the 1949 Act defines the protections to extend to "the appearance of the whole or part of a product resulting from the features of, in particular, the lines, contours, colours, shapes, texture or materials of the product or of its ornamentation". What is protected by registered designs, then, are aspects of the distinctive look and feel of the article and its packaging. As a result of this definition, aesthetic aspects of a product are most likely to be protected as registered designs. Courts used to judge the relevant qualities on the basis of "eye appeal" to the informed user (a person who is familiar with the field of design concerned). However, nowadays the courts acknowledge that both look and feel are important.

The protection is not automatic, unlike copyright, but requires to be applied for. The application for a registered design will therefore disclose all the distinctive features of the look and feel of the design. It is necessary that the application provides adequate specification. It is necessary to show that the design has (s 1B) both novelty and individual character. "Novelty" means that no materially identical design has been made available to the public before the application date. For these purposes, a design is not novel if it has been disclosed by publication, exhibition or use in trade prior to the application date. But this does not apply if the disclosure is made by the applicant within 12 months prior to the application date. "Individual character" relates to the distinctive impression the design has, as to its look and feel, on an informed user. However, the degree of creative freedom of the designer is also taken into account. Aspects of the design which are imposed upon the product are not protectable. For this reason, a design will not be protected where features of its look and feel are dictated solely by the need to achieve some technical function (s 1C). In addition, any feature of the products which is dictated by a need to connect to, in, around or against another product in order that the product or the other product performs its function will be excluded. This last restriction on design freedom is called a "must fit" exclusion and is of considerable importance. Apart from these restrictions, other aspects of the product may be registrable. A design will, however, not be protectable if it offends against public policy or morality. For example, the use of national emblems (national and Royal flags and emblems, the Crown, suggestions of Royal patronage, the Olympic symbol etc) as part of a design is a ground for refusal.

As with other forms of registrable intellectual property protection, the outcome of a successful application is the grant of a monopoly period of commercial exploitation. The monopoly period lasts for 5 years but this can be renewed on payment of the appropriate fee for a further four 5-year periods. In total, then, a registered design can have a monopoly of 25 years. The protection is granted to the designer (or their employer or commissioner if the design is created in the course of employment or is the outcome of a commission).

During the monopoly period, the design is infringed where a person, without the permission of the owner of the design, makes the product, offers or puts the product on the market, imports or exports the product, uses the product, or stocks the product for commercial purposes (s 7). The usual protections apply of interdict, damages, accounting for profit, and delivery up and destruction of infringing items. Because the owner must establish in an action of infringement that the infringer had the requisite knowledge, it is a defence (s 9) where an infringer establishes that they did so innocently and was not aware and had no reason to believe that the infringing product was registered. Section 26 provides any person groundlessly threatened with infringement proceedings to apply to the court for relief in the form of a declaration that the threats are unjustifiable, interdict (injunction) against the continuance of such threats, and damages for any loss incurred.

There are a number of non-commercial actions which do not constitute infringements (s 7A). These include: acts done privately and for non-commercial purposes; acts done for experimental purposes; acts done for teaching; the use of equipment on ships and aircraft registered outwith the UK but which are temporarily here; the importation of spare parts or accessories for use in repairing such ships or aircraft; the carrying out of such repairs; and the use (which includes producing and sale) of spare parts of complex products in order to carry out repairs to the complex product in such a way as to restore it to its original appearance. This last "spare parts" exception is one of considerable importance and with a long history in connection with both registered and unregistered designs.

UNREGISTERED DESIGN RIGHT

Unregistered designs are covered by ss 213–264 of the Copyright, Designs and Patents Act 1988. Unregistered design rights arise automatically (just as for copyright). No official disclosure of the design is required and there is no monopoly period in which the designer has exclusive right to exploit the design. Instead the prohibition is against copying a design. And any action of infringement involves some of the same difficulties of proof of ownership as we saw with copyright.

Unregistered design protection extends to any "original design" and protects in that design the "design of any aspect of the shape or configuration (whether internal or external) of the whole or part of an article" (s 213(2)). This definition means that the whole or any part of an original product, including its internal workings, can be protected even if the protected features are invisible to the human eye or totally enclosed within the product. As a result, unregistered design right is a much more important means of protecting the functional or technical aspects of a product.

"Original" means any design which is the original work of the designer and is therefore not commonplace in the design field at the time of creation. The meaning was tested in the case of *Farmers Build Ltd* v *Carier Bulk Materials Handling Ltd* (1999), which involved a slurry separator which separated manure into solid and liquid fractions. The defendants made their own separator with almost identical functional internal parts and it was therefore claimed that they had infringed the plaintiffs' design. The defendants claimed that the plaintiffs had done no more than recombine existing commonplace components well known in the field of agricultural machinery and so the overall design was commonplace and not original. The court formed the view that while some of the components could be regarded as commonplace in the field of agricultural machinery, nevertheless, the correct field to consider was that of slurry separators and in that restricted field the combination of internal parts was original. As a result the plaintiffs' separator had been the first in that field to combine the components together and so their design was not commonplace and was protected. If it is to be protected, a design must not have been copied from an earlier article. To decide whether the article is original it will be compared with other products in the same field. The court will carry out the comparison as a matter of fact and degree. The closer the similarity of designs in a relevant field, the more likely it is that the design features will be regarded as commonplace.

However, just as for registered designs, those parts of the design which are not part of the designer's creative freedom are excluded. Four matters are excluded from protection (s 213(3)): a method or principle of construction; "must fit" elements which enable the product to be connected to, or placed in, around or against, another article so that either article can perform its function; "must match" elements which are dependent upon the appearance of another article of which the first article is intended by the designer to form an integral part; and surface decoration.

For any form of design right to subsist, the design must have been recorded in some permanent form. In the case of a registered design, of course, the record is the application. In the case of an unregistered design, it is usual for a court to consider the original design drawings, design documents and prototype models. It is necessary to prove the authorship and date of these. A disclosure of the design as simply a collection of ideas is insufficient to establish what features are protected, since the ideas alone would lack specification.

Once more, it is the designer who is the first owner of a design, unless the designer was employed or his work has been commissioned, in which case the employer or commissioner is the first owner. The owner of the design right has the exclusive right to produce and exploit a design for commercial purposes. It is therefore a primary infringement of the design (s 226) to reproduce the design by making articles to the design or by making a design document recording the design for the purpose of enabling the designed articles to be made. It is also a primary infringement to authorise another person to reproduce the design without the authority of the owner. Secondary infringement occurs where, without the permission of the owner, infringing articles are imported or dealt with for commercial gain (s 227).

There are exceptions to design rights infringement where there also exist copyright protections in the design and the infringement is an infringement of the copyright (s 236). It appears that copyright protections take precedence over design right protections. In the last 5 years of protection, any person can reproduce a design under a licence of right, the terms of which will be settled by the comptroller (s 237). In certain circumstances (defence, and health purposes) the Crown may do any act which might infringe design right on payment of compensation for loss of profit (ss 240 and 243).

Remedies are dealt with in ss 229–231 and 233. Section 229 states that "relief by way of damages, injunctions, accounts or otherwise is available to the plaintiff". Section 230 gives the court the power to order delivery up of any infringing article. Section 231 gives the court the power to order forfeiture or destruction of infringing articles. Section 233 provides that where a defendant has innocently acquired infringing articles then the plaintiff's remedy will be restricted to damages not exceeding a reasonable royalty for the act complained of. Section 253 gives a remedy in respect of groundless threats of infringement proceedings.

Unregistered design right lasts for 10 years from the date of the first marketing of a product (or 15 years from the time when the design was first recorded in a design document).

SEMICONDUCTOR TOPOGRAPHY RIGHTS

Computer chips are now in very common use, not only in computers themselves but also in everyday items such as cars, washing machines and central heating controllers. This has meant that the computer chip market has grown exponentially and has for some time been the subject of special controls to prevent unfair competition.

Computer chips take huge amounts of time, effort and resources to design and producers are anxious to protect their chip "architecture". As a result, the design documents are protected, as also are the design elements of the chip and the "masks" (or etching stencils) used to reproduce the chips. In manufacture, silicon leaves are repeatedly etched with acid applied to the surface through masks. When the etching is complete, the surface of the silicon is etched with a distinctive microscopic pattern of pits and tracks to which metal terminals and wires are attached. The resultant chip is then encased in plastic.

The protections are provided by the Directive on Semiconductor Topographies (87/54/EC) which has been incorporated into UK law as the Design Right (Semiconductor Topographies) Regulations 1989 (SI 1989/1100). The design right subsists for 10 years from the end of the year when articles were first made using the topography (or 15 years from the time when the topography was first recorded in a design document). The protections extend to: "the pattern fixed, or intended to be fixed, in or upon a layer of semiconductor product, or a layer of material in the course of and for the purpose of the manufacture of a semiconductor product, or the arrangement of the patterns fixed, or intended to be fixed, in or upon the layers of a semiconductor product" (reg 2).

Regulation 8 (substituting a new s 226 into the Copyright, Designs and Patents Act 1988) states that the owner has the exclusive right to reproduce articles to the design or make a design document recording the design for the purpose of enabling articles to be made. But there is no infringement where the design is reproduced privately for non-commercial aims or for analysing or evaluating or teaching the concepts, processes, systems or techniques embodied in it.

Such analysis is very important when a manufacturer is evaluating chips for use in machinery and needs to understand the computer chip architecture. It would be a severe hurdle if such analysis were regarded as an infringement. Competitor chip manufacturers may therefore also analyse and evaluate a computer chip in order to understand its programming (the concepts, processes, systems or techniques embodied in it). The new s 226(4) specifically states that it is not an infringement of the design right to "create another original semiconductor topography as a result of an analysis or evaluation of the first topography or the concepts, processes, systems or techniques embodied in it, or to reproduce that other topography".

Essential Facts

Registered designs

- UK registered designs are protected under the Registered Designs Act 1949, as amended by the Copyright, Designs and Patents Act 1988 and the Registered Design Regulations 2001 and 2003. The protections extend to "the appearance of the whole or part of a product resulting from the features on, in particular, the lines, contours, colours, shapes, texture or materials of the product or of its ornamentation". What is protected by registered designs, then, are aspects of the distinctive look and feel of the article and its packaging.

- The protection requires to be applied for in an application that discloses all the distinctive features of the look and feel of the design. The design must have both novelty and individual character. "Novelty" means that no materially identical design has been made available to the public before the application date. "Individual character" relates to the distinctive impression the design has, as to its look and feel, on an informed user.

- A design will not be protected where features of its look and feel are dictated solely by the need to achieve some technical function, where the product "must fit" to another article, or if it offends against public policy or morality.

- A registered design can have a monopoly of 25 years. During the monopoly period, the design is infringed when any unauthorised person makes the product, offers or puts the product on the market, imports or exports the product, uses the product, or stocks the product for commercial purposes.

- Certain acts do no amount to infringement. These include acts done privately and for non-commercial purposes; experimental purposes; teaching; certain acts relating to repairs of ships and aircraft registered outwith the UK but which are temporarily here; and certain acts relating to spare parts.

Unregistered design right

- Unregistered designs are covered by ss 213–264 of the Copyright, Designs and Patents Act 1988 and involve automatic rights protecting any original design of any aspect of the shape or configuration (whether internal or external) of the whole or part of an article. This definition can therefore protect functional and technical aspects of a product.

- Four matters excluded from protection are: a method or principle of construction; "must fit" elements that enable the product to be connected to, or placed in, around or against, another article so that either article can perform its function; "must match" elements that are dependent upon the appearance of another article of which the first article is intended by the designer to form an integral part; and surface decoration.

- It is primary infringement to reproduce the design by making articles to the design or by making a design document recording the design for the purpose of enabling the designed articles to be made. Secondary infringement occurs where infringing articles are imported or dealt with.

- Unregistered design right lasts for 10 years from the date of the first marketing of a product (or 15 years from the time when the design was first recorded in a design document).

Semiconductor topography rights

- These are protected by the Design Right (Semiconductor Topographies) Regulations 1989 (SI 1989/1100). The design right subsists for 10 years from the end of the year when articles were first made using the topography (or 15 years from the time when the topography was first recorded in a design document). The protections extend to "the pattern fixed, or intended to be fixed, in or upon a layer of semiconductor product, or a layer of material in the course of and for the purpose of the manufacture of a semiconductor product, or the arrangement of the patterns fixed, or intended to be fixed, in or upon the layers of a semiconductor product".

- The owner has the exclusive right to reproduce articles to the design or make a design document recording the design for the purpose of enabling articles to be made. But there is no infringement where the design is reproduced privately for non-commercial aims or for analysing or evaluating or teaching the concepts, processes, systems or techniques embodied in it.

Essential Cases

Farmers Build Ltd v Carier Bulk Materials Handling Ltd (1999): this case involved a slurry separator which separated manure into solid and liquid fractions. The defendants claimed that the plaintiffs had done no more than recombine existing commonplace components well known in the field of agricultural machinery and so the overall design was commonplace and not original. The court formed the view that while some of the components could be regarded as commonplace in the field of agricultural machinery, nevertheless, the correct field to consider was that of slurry separators and in that restricted field the combination of internal parts was original. The plaintiffs' design was not commonplace and was protected. Generally, therefore, in order to decide whether the article is original, it will be compared with other products in the same field. The court will carry out the comparison as a question of fact and degree.

5 PATENTS

Patents are the oldest form of intellectual property rights, deriving from a time when the Crown gave monopoly rights to favoured individuals by means of Letters Patent. All sorts of monopolies could be given and the use of such patronage was not restricted to inventions. When it became clear that Crown patronage was being abused, Parliament passed the Statute of Monopolies of 1623 which placed limits on the rights which could be given. Today, inventions are given protection by means of patents. The current statute is the Patents Act 1977, as amended.

General

A patent is a monopoly right which lasts for 20 years (25 years in the case of pharmaceutical patents where research and development investment is considerable). Patents are protected inventions (whether products or processes) which (s 1(1)):

1. are new or novel;
2. involve an inventive step;
3. are capable of industrial application; and
4. are not excluded.

Generally, matters which are excluded are (by ss 1(2) and (3)):

1. a discovery, scientific theory or mathematical method;
2. a literary, dramatic, musical or artistic work or any other aesthetic creation (which is protected under copyright);
3. a scheme, rule or method for performing a mental act, playing a game or doing business, or a computer program;
4. the presentation of information (which may also be protected under copyright);
5. certain biotechnological inventions which are detailed in Sch 2A to the Act.

It is generally thought that the excluded matters (1) and (3) above involve categories of knowledge which are socially or economically valuable to society as a whole and therefore not matters which should be made the subject of a grant of monopoly in favour of an individual which would therefore give an unfair commercial advantage to the monopoly rights holder.

Biotechnological exclusions are justified on the bases of public policy and morality. They involve such matters as the human body in its various stages of formation and development; human cloning; human genetic identity modification processes; the use of human embryos for industrial commercial purposes; plant and animal varieties (which may have other forms of protection such as the Plant Varieties Act 1997); and the genetic modification of animals such as is likely to cause material suffering without any substantial medical benefit (an example of a case where this was argued is *Harvard Onco Mouse* (1991) where medical researchers introduced a gene into mouse DNA, giving rise to a variety of genetically modified mouse which had an increased likelihood of developing tumours, thus making it very useful for cancer research. In defending the patent, the Technical Board of Appeal made "a careful weighing up of the suffering of animals and possible risks to the environment on the one hand, and the inventions' usefulness to mankind on the other").

The "as such" rule

While the above excluded matters cannot be patented "as such", patent law does allow patents to be granted where these patents merely use an excluded matter to make a technical contribution to the working of the invention. This relaxation does not appear to extend to excluded biotechnological matters.

As a result of the "as such" rule, in *Merrill Lynch's application* (1989), a program on a computer which enabled markets to be created was held as unacceptable for patenting. The patent involved two excluded matters: a computer program and a method of doing business. It was argued that it would not necessarily have been excluded on the basis of using a computer program, since the program merely had technical effect. The use of a computer program "as such" is not patentable, but its use in a patent in order to achieve a necessary technical effect does not prevent the patent from being granted, provided that the result performs some purpose that is itself not excluded. In Merrill Lynch's case the patent was refused because its ultimate purpose was to give a means of doing business which was also an excluded matter.

In *IBM's application* (1999), a computer program had the technical effect of managing Windows applications and this was held to be capable of protection. It should be noted that the European Patent Office is more liberal than the UK Patent Office in its interpretation of "technical contribution".

Novelty

A patent must be new and will not be granted where the enabling technology involved is already part of the "state of the art" nor must the invention have been disclosed or made available to the public anywhere in the world in any way. Every patent application will be judged by asking whether the invention is novel by reference to the state of the art at the time of the application (the "priority date").

Disclosure of the invention, which would make it part of the "state of the art", and thus disqualify it from being granted, may occur in a number of ways. Three in particular are of note:

1. *Publication*: where the invention and the way that it is to be used have been disclosed to the public in published sources, journals, books or articles, or even where the inventor has made disclosures by demonstrations of the invention. These disqualifying publications can occur anywhere in the world and will prevent a patent from being regarded as a novel.

2. An *earlier* patent application (even if submitted only a few days earlier) will prevent a later application which uses the same enabling technology from being regarded as novel. However, the earlier application must contain "enabling information", which means that it must disclose sufficiently how the patent works and also how it is to be applied and used.

3. *Use*: the principle is that it is not proper to apply for and obtain a monopoly where the product or process is something which is or has already been made or done by other people. A very good example here is the case of *Windsurfing International Inc* v *Tabur Marine (GB) Ltd* (1985), which involved a 12-year-old boy who had anticipated Windsurfing International's wishbone spar surfboard patent application by having used the same type of surfboard in public a number of years prior to the application. The court was able to view a film of his early use of this off the Isle of Wight. The disclosure meant that the invention was sufficiently disclosed at the time of the application and therefore the application had to be refused.

   Earlier uses will not necessarily disqualify an invention unless the disclosure is sufficient to provide information about how the invention works and is applied or used ("enabling disclosure"), so that in the case of *PLG Research Ltd* v *Ardon International* (1995), the earlier use did not disqualify. The question of enabling disclosure was also raised in *Mobil/friction reducing additive* (1990), where it was held that a new use for an existing product can give rise to a new patent. Prior uses will invalidate an application if the use disclosed there shows how the invention works. This gives rise to the concept of an "enabling use". In the *Mobil* case the product had been used previously, to prevent rusting, but it was discovered that a new use would prevent friction in addition thereby making engines more efficient. The new use was sufficient to enable a new patent to be granted.

Inventive step

An invention is required to show an inventive step which is "not obvious to a person skilled in the art, having regard to any matter which forms part of the state of the art" (s 3). This has given rise to a number of questions about what is "obvious" and what is not, and to whom the inventive step must be obvious.

To whom must the inventive step be obvious? In *Technograph Printed Circuits Ltd* v *Mills & Rockley (Electronics) Ltd* (1972), the court held that the person to whom a patent must be obvious is "a skilled but unimaginative worker". The requisite level of skill and imagination will vary from application to application.

How do the courts go about deciding what the inventive step is and whether it is obvious? In *Windsurfing International* the court gave a four-step procedure:

i.   identify the inventive concept;

ii. what was the general knowledge in the state of the art at the priority date (date of application)?

iii. what is the difference between the matter cited in the alleged invention and the general knowledge in the state of the art at the priority date?

iv. are these steps obvious to the skilled man?

It can be seen that this gives rise to a number of issues. Courts have often asked why, if something is obvious, it has not been done before. This is known as the "problem of hindsight". A number of cases illustrate this:

Parks Kramer Co v *G W Thornton & Sons Ltd* (1966) this involved a vacuum tube suspended from the ceiling of a factory, the tube being used to suck up fluff. This technical solution appeared obvious with the benefit of hindsight but until the patent application had been made there had been an unfulfilled need in the industry. Mills had a problem with fluff and the invention solved the problem and was a proven commercial success.

Haberman v *Jackal International Ltd* (1999), involved the "Anyway Up" cup used by babies. The problem was that babies often dropped what they were drinking and spilt the contents of their cups but the invention was a cup with a very small slit in a mouthpiece which allowed water and other liquids to escape only when there was sucking action. This meant that when the cup was dropped, the liquids wouldn't spill out. This was the first patent application to deal with this particular problem.

Ownership

We saw in relation to copyright that the owner is usually the creator of the idea concerned. With patents, the ownership is usually vested in the inventor but there are exceptions to this. One very important category of exception relates to employees. Usually, if a person is employed as an inventor and resources are made available to them, the patents in the inventions will accrue to the employer. But not all inventions invented by employees will be owned by the employer. Employers will have rights where the invention is made in the course of the employee's normal employment duties. It is therefore important to look to the employee's contract of employment so as to decide whether or not they are required to invent in order to fulfil their duties. In other cases, it will be necessary to look at a number of other criteria which may indicate that the employer expects invention rights to accrue to them. Such criteria may include whether resources or time have been made available to the employee to carry out inventing in company time and on company premises. If an employer provides equipment or finance to fund inventing then that might indicate that the employer intends the employee to invent as part of their duties.

In *Electrolux* v *Hudson* (1977), Hudson was employed as a storekeeper. His duties did not involve inventing at all – he was simply a storekeeper – but because of his familiarity with his employers' products he was able to invent a new kind of universal connector. It was held that his invention could not be regarded as being made during the course of his employment and so it was owned by him and not by his employers. His employment duties to his employer were held to be restricted to selling items and dealing with their stores.

In *Greater Glasgow Health Board application* (1996), an ophthalmologist invented a device which assisted him in carrying out clinical examinations and diagnoses. The health board claimed the ownership of the invention but the doctor was able to satisfy the court that he would not have breached his employment duties had he not made the invention at all, he was not required to invent, and as a result the invention was his property.

Section 40 of the 1977 Act allows an employee to claim compensation where their invention is of outstanding benefit to an employer – but it must be something quite out of the ordinary. The court must be satisfied that compensation should justly be awarded. There are various grounds. In practice it is difficult to obtain statutory compensation.

Dealings in patents

Just as with copyright, the owner of a patent can assign, mortgage, transfer and license his rights. It is usual for such dealings to be in writing and to be signed by the owner of the rights concerned. A person to whom a patent is transferred should register their interest on the Patents Register.

Applications

When a person wishes to have a patent, he must make an application on the prescribed form and must include a number of documents (s 14*ff*). These documents are:

1. the *abstract*: this is a very brief description of the invention and how it works. The reason for the abstract is to give notice of the application in the *Official Journal* at the time when the application is first lodged.
2. the *specification*: this contains the technical drawings and technical description of the patent, stating how the patented article or process is made, how it works and what its functional components are.
3. the *claims*: these constitute the legal description of what is claimed as a monopoly.

The application must be accompanied by the appropriate fee. The application process involves a preliminary search and thereafter a full search in order to assess whether the patent fulfils all the criteria given in s 1(1) and has not been disclosed prior to the priority date (the date of the application). Even after the patent is granted, it may be challenged. This may occur in the course of an action taken by the patent owner against an alleged infringer.

An important case is that of *Catnic Components Ltd* v *Hill & Smith Ltd* (1982), which involved a lifting device. The original application had a vertical load-bearing component, while the application of the alleged infringer had a closely similar device for load lifting but which had a slightly inclined load-bearing component. This varied from the original application by merely 6 degrees. The court had to decide whether or not the variant was materially different and affected the invention and so formulated three questions:

1. does the variant materially affect the operation of the invention?
2. is it obvious to the skilled reader that the variant has no material effect?
3. is strict compliance with the legal claims made by the original applicant essential?

The European Patent Office has proved much more liberal in its interpretation of patent applications than the British Office, where a much stricter and more literal approach has been taken. For example, in the case of *Union Carbide* v *BP Chemicals* (1999), the court held that the monopoly fell between the extremes of a literal construction (as would be used in the United Kingdom) and the use of claims as a guideline. In *Consafe Engineering UK Ltd* v *Emitunga UK Ltd* (1999), the issue was whether the patent applicant intended that a precise word or phrase was an essential requirement of the invention.

Infringement

Infringement is dealt with in ss 60–71 of the 1977 Act. "Primary infringement" is the most important form and is of three sorts:

1. where product patents are at issue, infringement involves the making, disposing of, using, importing or keeping the patented product;
2. where a patented process is involved, infringement involves the use of the process with the natural or constructive knowledge that non-consensual or unauthorised use constitutes infringement;
3. in both cases the use, offer to dispose of, importation or keeping for disposal or otherwise of a product directly obtained from a patented process.

There is also "contributory infringement" which is the supply or offer to supply any of the means that relate to an essential element of an invention.

There are exceptions to infringement which involve private and non-commercial uses and experimental uses. In both of these the party who is "infringing" the patent is not doing so for any commercial gain. The courts consider that repairs to patented products, where there is a clear and genuine repair, does not constitute an infringement.

Other than these, there are a number of other minor categories of non-commercial use which do not infringe patents and which are detailed in s 60(5)(a) and (i) of the Act.

Defences

A wide range of defences is open in any claim of infringement. For example, the infringer can:

1. challenge the patents: they could say that the invention is not patentable, that the patentee was not entitled to a patent, that the specification was not sufficiently clear and full, the specification went beyond the application, or that an amendment has extended the patent which was allowed;
2. claim that there has been no infringement;
3. claim certain statutory defences – for example, that the infringing activity was private and non-commercial, was carried out for experimental purposes, etc;
4. claim that the patent rights have been exhausted;
5. claim that the infringement was in good faith and in continuation of an activity done since before the priority (application) date; and
6. claim that there is an implied licence.

Remedies

These include:

1. declarator that the patent has been infringed;
2. injunction or interdict – to prevent a repetition of the infringing activity;
3. order for recovery and destruction of infringing articles;
4. damages for losses incurred by the patent rights holder;
5. accounting for recovery of any profits made by the infringer.

Licences of right and compulsory licences

A patent owner may work the patent themselves or may agree privately to license third parties to work the patent. The patent owner, if they do not wish to work the patent themselves, can place an entry on the register, stating that licences of right are available. This publicises the fact that licences are available and will be granted on application on reasonable terms. Where the terms cannot be agreed by private agreement, the patent owner or the third party can apply to the Comptroller to fix the terms.

Where the patent has been granted for over 3 years and the patent owner is not working the patent to its full potential but has refused to grant a licence to a third party on reasonable terms, the third party can apply to the Comptroller for a compulsory licence. The precise grounds are set out in s 48.

Essential Facts

- Patents are one of the oldest forms of monopoly right. They derive from Crown patronage where monopolies in trade were granted by the Crown to favoured individuals. Patents are now restricted to invented products and processes and are granted following application to the Patent Office.
- Patents can be granted only where the four criteria in s 1(1) of the Patents Act 1977 are fulfilled. The product or process must: be new or novel; involve an inventive step; be capable of industrial application; and not be excluded.
- Patents cannot be granted for excluded matters "as such". Excluded matters include: discoveries; scientific theories; mathematical methods; schemes, rules or methods for performing a mental act, playing a game or doing business; computer programs; certain biotechnological inventions; and certain matters which have other forms of intellectual property protection.
- Patents which merely use an excluded matter to give a technical contribution or achieve a technical effect can be granted.
- *Novelty*: a patent must be new and will not be granted where the enabling technology involved is already part of the "state of the art"; neither must the invention have been disclosed or made available to the public anywhere in the world in any way. Disqualifying disclosures may occur by prior publication, use or application where the disclosure sufficiently specifies what the invention is, how it works and how it is to be used.
- *Inventive step*: a patent must be "not obvious to a person skilled in the art, having regard to any matter which forms part of the state of

the art". The person skilled in the art is "a skilled but unimaginative worker". The requisite level of skill and imagination will vary from application to application. In *Windsurfing International* the court gave a four-step procedure for deciding what the inventive step was and stating whether it was obvious to the skilled man.

- *Hindsight*: sometimes a patent which gives a solution to a technical problem appears obvious in hindsight. But where the problem has existed for some time without a solution being available, this suggests that at the time of the patent application the solution was not obvious.

- *Ownership*: the inventor is usually the owner of the patent. Employers may have right to patents where the employee works under a contract which states that his or her duties include inventing or when resources or time have been made available to the employee to carry out inventing in company time and on company premises.

- The owner of a patent can assign, mortgage, transfer and license their rights. It is usual for such dealings to be in writing.

- When a person wishes to have a patent, they must make an application on the prescribed form and must include a number of documents. These documents are: the abstract (which is a very brief description of the invention and how it works) which is used to give notice of the patent application; the specification (which contains the technical drawings and technical description of the patent stating how the patented article or process is made, how it works and what its functional components are); and the claims (these constitute the legal description of what is claimed as a monopoly). One important role for the claims is that they will be used to decide whether any subsequent patent application involves a fresh inventive step or is merely a variant of the patent previously granted.

- Primary infringement of a patent occurs: where the infringer makes, imports, uses, keeps, or disposes of a patented product without authorisation; where the infringer makes unauthorised use of a patented process; or where the infringer uses, keeps, imports or disposes of a product of a patented process without authorisation. There is a wide range of defences open to an alleged infringer. This could include challenging the validity of the patent.

- Licences may be agreed privately or, when a licence of right has been publicised and no agreement has been reached, the Comptroller will fix the terms of the licence. Where the patent has been granted for over 3 years and the patent owner is not working the patent to its full potential but has refused to grant a licence to a third party on reasonable terms, the third party can apply to the Comptroller for a compulsory licence. The precise grounds are set out in s 48.

Essential Cases

Harvard Onco Mouse (1991): medical researchers introduced a gene into mouse DNA, giving rise to a variety of genetically modified mouse which had an increased likelihood of developing tumours, thus making it very useful for cancer research. In defending the patent, the Technical Board of Appeal made "a careful weighing up of the suffering of animals and possible risks to the environment on the one hand, and the inventions' usefulness to mankind on the other".

Merrill Lynch's application (1989): a computer program which enabled markets to be created was held to be unacceptable for patenting. The patent involved two excluded matters: a computer program and a method of doing business. The use in a patent of a computer program to achieve a necessary technical effect does not prevent the patent from being granted. In this case the patent was refused because its ultimate purpose was to give a means of doing business, which was another excluded matter.

IBM's application (1999): a computer program had the technical effect of managing Windows applications and this was held to be capable of protection.

Windsurfing International Inc v Tabur Marine (GB) Ltd (1985): a 12-year-old boy anticipated Windsurfing International's wishbone spar surfboard patent by having used the same type of surfboard in public a number of years prior to the application. The court was able to view a film of his early use of this off the Isle of Wight. The disclosure meant that the invention was sufficiently disclosed at the time of the application and therefore the application had to be refused.

Mobil/friction reducing additive (1990): held that a new use for an existing product can give rise to a new patent. The product had been used previously in order to prevent rusting but it was discovered that a new use could prevent friction in addition, thereby making engines more efficient. The new use was sufficient to enable a new patent to be granted.

Technograph Printed Circuits Ltd v Mills & Rockley (Electronics) Ltd (1972): held that the person to whom a patent must be obvious is "a skilled but unimaginative worker".

Parks Kramer Co v G W Thornton & Sons Ltd (1966): a vacuum tube suspended from the ceiling of a factory was used to suck up fluff. Until the patent application had been made there had been an unfulfilled need in the industry. The solution might appear to be obvious with the benefit of hindsight, but while the problem persisted, the solution had not suggested itself.

Haberman v Jackal International Ltd (1999): this involved the "Anyway Up" cup used by babies. The problem was that babies often dropped what they were drinking and spilt the contents of their cups but the invention was a cup with a very small slit in a mouthpiece which allowed only water and other liquids to escape when there was sucking action. This meant that when the cup was dropped the liquids wouldn't spill out. This was the first patent application to deal with this particular problem. The solution only appears obvious with the benefit of hindsight.

Electrolux v Hudson (1977): Hudson was employed as a storekeeper. His duties did not involve invention at all but because of his familiarity with his employers' products he was able to invent a new kind of universal connector. Held that his invention could not be regarded as being made during the course of his employment and so it was owned by him and not by his employers. His employment duties to his employer were held to be restricted to selling items and dealing with their stores.

Greater Glasgow Health Board application (1996): an ophthalmologist invented a device which assisted him in carrying out clinical examinations and diagnoses. The health board claimed ownership of the invention but the doctor was able to satisfy the court that he would not have breached his employment duties had he not made the invention at all, he was not required to invent, and as a result the invention was his property.

Catnic Components Ltd v Hill & Smith Ltd (1982): this case involved a lifting device. The original application had a vertical load-bearing component, while the application of the alleged infringer had a closely similar device for load lifting but which differed by having a slightly inclined load-bearing component. This varied from the original application by a mere 6 degrees. The court had to decide whether or not the variant was materially different and affected the invention.

6 TRADE MARKS

Registered and unregistered trade marks and brands

Trade mark protections historically arose in the mid-19th century when it became clear that a trader's name and logo applied to goods could become distinctive brands and have an economic value. They inspired customer loyalty and could be used as a mark of quality or origin. It was clear that there was a need for some form of legal recognition and protection in order to prevent rogue traders from passing themselves off as the true owners of the trade marks concerned.

One way of doing this was for a trader to establish a reputation during the course of trade and to build up a connection in the minds of customers between the trader's distinctive mark and their goods and services. Such customer loyalty can be seen as a form of goodwill. Unregistered brands created in this way are an automatic right arising purely from trade usage by the owner. To protect these unregistered brands from being trespassed upon by other traders, it is necessary for the true owner to raise an action against an infringer under the common law of passing off (for which see Chapter 7). The difficulty in the case of unregistered marks is that within the court action the owner has to prove ownership of the brand: he has to prove the established use of the mark; that the mark is unique or a least well known in the trader's distinctive sector; that the mark is recognised by the trader's consumers and by other traders; that the infringer has used the mark to gain sales on the basis of confusion with the goods of the true owner of the mark; and, finally, that the true owner of the brand has thereby lost revenue.

Another way to protect brands was for the Government to establish a system of registered trade marks where issues of ownership and recognition of a brand, and thus sole entitlement to use it, were assumed following registration. Registered marks require to be applied for using a statutory applications procedure followed by a search to establish distinctiveness of the mark in the sector of trade concerned. Because ownership and use are assumed, actions by registered trade mark holders are therefore fewer in number and considerably shorter in terms of court time and resources expended.

Registered trade marks as graphically represented signs

A preliminary difficulty with registered trade marks is how they are to be defined. In the Trade Marks Act 1994, s 1(1) defines a trade mark as "any sign capable of being represented graphically which is capable of distinguishing the goods or services of one undertaking from those of another" and which "may, in particular, consist of words (including personal names), designs, letters, numerals or the shape of goods or their packaging". The sign requires to be capable of graphic representation because, in a system of registered marks, the trade mark application and grant must adequately specify by means of drawings, graphics or print the distinctive mark which is to be used. The means of specification must be sufficient to indicate to any competitor reading the application or grant what it is that they must refrain from using in relation to their own goods and services. There should also be no scope for confusion by customers.

Given the above definition, there is scope for registering many forms of distinctive "signs". The courts have therefore built up a considerable body of case law, with some issues being particularly important. Four such areas stand out for special consideration:

Shapes

The 1994 Act (for the first time in the UK) allowed shapes to be protected as trade marks (s 1(1)). An example of this kind of trade mark is the Coca-Cola bottle which is moulded in the form of a stylised cola pod. Prior to the 1994 Act, the Coca-Cola Company had tried repeatedly and unsuccessfully to protect their bottle shape in the UK but the courts had always refused to allow this. Though the courts were interpreting the previous statutory provisions, they expressed their reluctance by saying that to protect packaging would allow dealing or trafficking in the trade mark as a commodity in its own right (prohibited under the 1938 Trade Marks Act). The current latitude does not mean that all shapes are protectable. Certain shapes are not capable of being trade marks. Such shapes are those which are functional or technical characteristics of the product. To give protection in such cases would give an unacceptable advantage to the trade mark owner, for it would effectively prevent competitors from taking advantage of the functional or technical aspects concerned. It is not the function of trade marks to frustrate functional and technological advances. In *Philips Electronics NV v Remington Consumer Products* (Case C–299/99) (2002), the court said that the reason for refusal to allow trade mark protection to a two-dimensional representation of a three headed-rotary shaver head was "to prevent trade mark protection from granting its proprietor a monopoly on technical solutions or functional characteristics of a product which a user is likely to seek in the products of a competitor". Shapes of products, or even of packing, can be trade marked within the constraints of reason.

Colours

This aspect became particularly important with drug capsules, some of which may gain global notoriety among consumers from their colours and shapes (for example Pfizer's "Viagra" pill). But in any trade mark application, the purpose of the colours must be to enable the consumer to recognise the product concerned rather than to achieve any other purpose (such as dosage). See *John Wyeth's Coloured Tablet Trade Mark* (1988). But in recent times, dubiety about how to specify colours has given rise to cases such as *Orange Personal Communications Ltd's application* (2000), where an attempt was made to trade mark a particular shade of orange and this was refused on the ground of insufficient specification of the colour concerned. The court held that since there were "unaccountable different numbers of shades" to which the use of the expression "orange" could refer, that expression did not provide sufficient information to state to the reader what precisely was protected.

Sounds and smells

The need for an unambiguous graphic representation has produced some difficulties too. In many cases, musical notation has been sufficient to protect a sound (because anyone who knows how to read the notation will be able to read from it the type of sound that is protected), but there are difficulties where the trader seeks to protect natural sounds which cannot be reduced to musical notation. In the case of smells, there are particular difficulties in specifying these. Individual chemical scents can be uniquely identified from their chemical formulae, for, theoretically, a chemist can go away and reproduce the chemical in his laboratory and so see what the protected odour smells like. But even the most informed chemist is unable to gain an insight into the smell from reading the written formula alone.

The issue for both sounds and smells, then, is how a graphic description can be made specific enough for it to be understandable to the educated reader and so utilisable as a trade mark. This is not to say that a verbal description is impossible but cases show how difficult it is. In *Vennootschap onder Firma Senta Aromatic Marketing's Application* (1999), an application was made to register the "smell of fresh cut grass" as a trade mark for a tennis ball manufacturer. The court held that the issue is always "whether or not this description gives clear enough information to those reading it to walk away with an immediate and unambiguous idea of what the mark is ... the smell of fresh cut grass is a distinct smell, which everyone immediately recognises from experience ... the Board is satisfied that the description provided for the olfactory mark sought to be registered for tennis balls is appropriate and complies with the graphical representation requirement". But in *John Lewis's application (scent of cinnamon)* (2001), an attempt to obtain a trade mark for the scent described as "fruity with a hint of cinnamon" was refused. In most cases the chemical formula of the scent and even a sample of the chemical will be insufficient, since this will not enable a person reading the graphical description to obtain any idea of what the trade mark is.

The essence of the graphically represented sign is that it must be capable of allowing the reader of the grant, as well as the consumer, to distinguish the goods and services of one business from those of another. This is not necessarily a high standard but it will obviously bar the use of any signs which are incapable of adequate specification, graphic representation and those that are physically incapable of functioning as a distinctive sign associated with products.

Trade marks applications subject to absolute refusal

Section 3 of the 1994 Act gives a set of trade marks which "shall not be registered". These include:

- *s 3(1)*: signs which do not satisfy the requirements of s 1(1); marks which are devoid of distinctive character; signs that are exclusively descriptive; and marks which consist exclusively of signs or indications which have become customary in the current language or in the established practices of the trade;
- *s 3(2)*: signs which result exclusively from the nature of the goods; or which are necessary to attain a technical result or shape which gives substantial value to the goods. We have seen an example of these above;
- *s 3(3)*: marks contrary to public policy or morality or intended to deceive the public;
- *s 3(4)*: marks prohibited by enactment or legal rule; or (s 3(5) and 4) certain specially protected emblems (such as the Royal arms, representations of members of the Royal family, suggestions as to Royal patronage, national flags and emblems, emblems of certain

international organisations (such as of the International Olympic Committee));

- *s 3(6)*: where an application is made in bad faith.

In addition to marks subject to absolute refusal, there are also marks which may be subject to relative refusal. Any mark which is the same as or similar to an existing registered mark in the same class of goods or services will be subject to such refusal. Schedule 4 to the Trade Marks Rules 2000 gives 34 classes of goods and 11 classes of services which may be identified in the application. The importance of classes will be illustrated in the case of *Oasis Store Ltd's Trade Mark application* (1998) which is referred to in the next paragraph. In each case the court must consider the similarity of the mark and the similarity of the product (see also "infringement" below). Both of these considerations introduce elements of subjectivity. In each case it is relevant to ask whether the consumer is likely to be confused by the later mark.

To take as an example of an objection where use classes became important, in *Oasis Store Ltd's Trade Mark application*, the store applied to register the trade mark "EVEREADY" for its range of contraceptives. The application was objected to by Every Ready plc, a manufacturer of batteries and electrical goods which suggested that there would be a real risk of confusion with its own products and a resulting deception of the consumer. The objection was overruled on a number of grounds: the goods were not of the same classes; there was therefore little risk of confusion among consumers; there was no suggestion that Ever Ready plc's reputation was being damaged or taken advantage of. The fact that goods and services are in different classes makes an objector's assertions more difficult to establish, since there is less likelihood of confusion of the public.

Signs that are devoid of distinctive character, or are descriptive or generic

As we have seen, any mark which is devoid of distinctive character is excluded from protection. A trade mark that involves a very common surname is unlikely to be distinctive. The same applies to common words: in *British Sugar v James Robertson (TREAT)* (1996), it was held that the sign "TREAT" was devoid of distinctive character. The intention had been to use this as a name for a syrup for pouring on ice creams and desserts. Such marks may, however, become distinctive by unregistered trade use for a sufficient period to enable consumer recognition over a period of time.

More specifically, this exclusion applies to any mark that is exclusively descriptive (as to "kind, quality, quantity, intended purpose, value, geographical origin, the time of production of goods or of rendering of services, or other characteristics of goods or services") or generic (such as the use of "personal" if applied to personal computers). Once again, the justification for exclusion is that these, like the technical and functional shapes referred to above, would give an unfair advantage to the trade mark owner if granted.

The registration procedure

For registered trade marks, the process of application for registration (s 32*ff*) involves the completion of an application form giving certain information about the identity and address of the applicant, a statement of the particular product or service to be protected, a graphical representation of the mark, and the statement that the mark is already being or is about to be used by the applicant. In addition the applicant needs to pay the fees for each class of goods or services with which it is intended to use the mark.

Following the application, a search and examination is made and notification of the application is published. Objections may be made within 3 months of publication. If no opposition is filed, the application will be granted. The grant of a trade mark satisfies the property assertions which we have seen before and which additionally have to be proved with an unregistered trade mark when raising an action of infringement. Trade mark protection lasts for 10 years and may be renewed for further periods of 10 years.

Just as a trade mark can be registered, so it can also be removed from the register in a number of circumstances (such as that it should never have been granted in the first place – which may be pled as a defence during infringement proceedings).

Infringement

Infringement (s 10) comprises the use of an identical sign for identical goods and services (ie goods and services in the same class); or an identical or similar sign with identical or similar goods and services; or use of a mark similar to a mark of repute with similar goods and services. A mark of repute is the mark of some organisation or body such as, for example, the Soil Association or the British Farmers' mark. "Use" means affixing the registered sign to goods or packaging; exposing such goods or packaging for sale; importing or exporting such goods; or using the sign on business papers or in advertising.

In deciding whether there has been infringement of a registered trade mark, the court must assess the *similarity of the mark* and so will look at the overall *impression* (the look of the mark, the sound of a name, the nature of the customers, and any other relevant circumstances). The question for the court is whether the use is normal and fair; whether there has been any deception by the owner; and whether the mark is recognised by a substantial number of people.

In assessing the *similarity of products*, the court will consider the nature and composition of goods; the markets used; the trade channels in which it is sold; and, in particular, whether confusion of the public may occur; the likelihood of confusion; the choice of the mark; the length of time the mark has been used; proof of the circumstances of any actual confusion that has occurred; the size of trade; and inconvenience to the parties.

Remedies and defences against groundless threats

The usual remedies apply (see previous chapters). In addition, there exist certain criminal offences relating to the falsification of an entry in the register; falsely representing that a mark has been registered; the using of a registered mark in an area where there is no authorised use class; and the unauthorised use of arms and other symbols.

As with patents, the defender in a trade mark infringement has a wide range of defences available, including challenging the grant of the trade mark (as in *Philips Electronics NV v Remington Consumer Products* (2002)). A trade mark is not infringed where there are two or more overlapping registrations; where the defender is using his own name or address; where there is a descriptive use; where the use is to indicate an intended purpose for the product; in comparative advertising; where there has been prior use by the defender; and in a number of other situations (see s 11).

Another important safeguard available to smaller traders is given in s 21 of the Act. This safeguard states that where in certain circumstances a person threatens another with proceedings for infringement of a registered trade mark, the party threatened may obtain certain remedies from the court. The remedies may comprise a declaration that the threats are unjustifiable; an injunction (interdict) against the continuance of the threats; and damages in respect of any loss the threatened party has sustained as a result of the threats. This protection is very useful, as large organisations with deep pockets could otherwise threaten the very existence of small trade competitors by means of repeated and unjustifiable threats which the small trader has few resources to defend.

Character merchandising

This occurs where goods are merchandised by means of association with a real or fictional character. Much of the protection of such characters depends on the law of passing off (for which see Chapter 7), but the central issue is whether the public would consider that there was a real association with the character concerned. In *Wombles Ltd* v *Wombles Skips Ltd* (1977), the case was raised by the owners of the rights in books, drawing and cartoons of the fictional characters who resided on Wimbledon Common and collected rubbish. The defendant was a skip hire company. The plaintiffs failed mainly because it was not considered that there was a common field of activity whereby a reasonable man might assume a connection. It was also important that it was only the name rather than images which were copied. Since that case there has been a move away from insistence that there must be a common field of activity for passing off. This is no doubt because real and fictional characters are now involved in the business of merchandising, often licensing others to carry out activities associating them with the character name and image as pieces of intellectual property. The high point was reached in the case of *Mirage Studios* v *Counter-Feat Clothing Co Ltd* (1991), in which the plaintiffs operated a business which included the licensing of the name and images of cartoon characters called "Teenage Mutant Ninja Turtles". They were able to prevent the defendants from selling clothing which displayed the graphic characters.

In the field of trade marks, however, protection of a character is not so easily acquired. In *Elvis Presley trade mark application* (1999), the applicants were unsuccessful in registering the names "Elvis" and "Elvis Presley": the court held that the public merely wanted to buy goods with the name or image on them and that (per Walker LJ) "the article on which the name or image appears ... is little more than a vehicle". These aspects had become descriptive within our culture and no longer indicated a real association with the singer. To register these names as trade marks would deny other traders the opportunity to use them as well.

Essential Facts

- Trade marks inspire customer loyalty and can be used as a mark of quality or origin.

- A trader can establish goodwill in a brand by building up a reputation during the course of trade and so making a connection in the minds of customers between the trader's distinctive mark and their goods and services. Unregistered brands created in this way are an automatic right arising purely from trade usage by the owner. The difficulty in the case of unregistered marks is that within the court action the owner has to prove ownership of the brand and established use as well as infringement and loss.

- Registered marks require to be applied for using a statutory application procedure followed by a search in order to establish distinctiveness of the mark in the sector of trade concerned. Registered trade mark owners do not have to prove ownership or use in infringement actions.

- A trade mark is "any sign capable of being represented graphically which is capable of distinguishing the goods or services of one undertaking from those of another" and which "may, in particular, consist of words (including personal names), designs, letters, numerals or the shape of goods or their packaging".

- Signs may include shapes, including the shapes of packaging. Shapes which give a functional or technical advantage to the applicant are not registrable, as they would prevent competitors from taking advantage of the functional or technical aspects concerned.

- Colours may be registered where the purpose of the colours is to enable the consumer to recognise the product concerned rather than to achieve any other purpose. As there are unaccountable different numbers of shades of colour, an applicant must provide sufficient information to state to the reader of the application and grant in order to know what precisely is protected.

- Sounds and smells may also suffer from difficulties in specifying the sound or smell in an unambiguous graphic representation. In some cases musical notation may be sufficient. Chemical formulas or samples of smells are not sufficient.

- Trade mark applications are subject to absolute refusal on grounds laid out in s 3 where they are devoid of distinctive character; purely descriptive; result exclusively from the nature of the goods; necessary to attain a technical result; give substantial value to the goods; are contrary to public policy or morality; are intended to deceive the public; are prohibited by enactment or legal rule; involve certain specially protected emblems; or where the application is made in bad faith.

- Trade marks may be subject to relative refusal where the mark is the same as or similar to an existing registered mark in the same class of goods or services.

- Schedule 4 to the Trade Marks Rules 2000 gives 34 classes of goods and 11 classes of services which may be identified in the application.

- The process of application for registration for a trade mark involves the completion of an application form giving prescribed information; a search and examination; and publication. Where no objections are made within 3 months of publication, the application will be granted.

- Infringement comprises the use of an identical sign for identical goods and services; or an identical or similar sign with identical or similar goods and services; or use of a mark similar to a mark of repute with similar goods and services. "Use" means affixing the registered sign to goods or packaging; exposing such goods or packaging for sale; importing or exporting such goods; or using the sign on business papers or in advertising. The court will assess the similarity of the mark by looking at the overall impression (the look of the mark, the sound of a name, the nature of the customers, and any other relevant circumstances). It is relevant whether any actual confusion of the public has occurred.

- In addition to the usual remedies, there exist certain criminal offences relating to the falsification of an entry in the register; the falsely representing that a mark has been registered; the using of a registered mark in an area where there is no authorised use class; and the unauthorised use of arms and other symbols.

- Character merchandising occurs where goods are merchandised by means of association with a real or fictional character. Much of the protection of such characters depends on the law of passing off but the central issue is whether the public would consider that there was a real association with the character concerned. In the field of trade marks, protection of a character may not be easily acquired where it can be shown that the mark has become descriptive and does not indicate a link to the original character.

Essential Cases

Philips Electronics NV v Remington Consumer Products (Case C–299/99) (2002): Philips had obtained trade mark protection for a two-dimensional representation of a three-headed rotary shaver head. Remington objected to the grant and was successful in having the trade mark removed from the register in order "to prevent trade mark protection from granting its proprietor a monopoly on technical solutions or functional characteristics of a product which a user is likely to seek in the products of a competitor".

Vennootschap onder Firma Senta Aromatic Marketing's Application (1999): an application to register the "smell of fresh cut grass" as a trade mark for a tennis ball manufacturer was held to give clear enough information to those reading it to walk away with an immediate and unambiguous idea of what the mark is.

John Lewis's application (scent of cinnamon) (2001): an attempt to obtain a trade mark for the scent described as "fruity with a hint of cinnamon" was refused.

Oasis Store Ltd's Trade Mark application (1998): the store applied to register the trade mark "EVEREADY" for its range of contraceptives. The application was objected to by Every Ready plc, a manufacturer of batteries and electrical goods, who suggested that there would be a real risk of confusion with its own products and a resulting deception of the consumer. The objection was overruled. The goods were not of the same classes; there was therefore little risk of confusion among consumers; there was no suggestion that Ever Ready plc's reputation was being damaged or taken advantage of.

British Sugar v James Robertson (TREAT) (1996): it was held that the sign "TREAT" was devoid of distinctive character. The intention had been to use this as a name for a syrup for pouring on ice creams and desserts. Such marks may, however, become distinctive by unregistered trade use for a sufficient period to enable consumer recognition over a period of time.

Wombles Ltd v Wombles Skips Ltd (1977): a case was raised by the owners of the rights in books, drawing and cartoons of the fictional characters who resided on Wimbledon Common and collected rubbish. The defendant was a skip hire company. The plaintiffs failed mainly because it was not considered that there was a common field of activity whereby a reasonable man might assume a connection.

Mirage Studios v Counter-Feat Clothing Co Ltd (1991): the plaintiffs operated a business which included the licensing of the name and images of cartoon characters called "Teenage Mutant Ninja Turtles". They were able to prevent the defendants from selling clothing which displayed the graphic characters.

Elvis Presley trade mark application (1999): the applicants were unsuccessful in registering the names "Elvis" and "Elvis Presley". The court held that the public merely wanted to buy goods with the name or image on them and that (per Walker LJ) "the article on which the name or image appears … is little more than a vehicle". These aspects had become descriptive within our culture and no longer indicated a real association with the singer.

7 PASSING OFF

Passing off occurs when one business falsely trades upon the confusion of its goods or services with those of a well-known competitor who has an established goodwill in the market concerned. That is to say that consumers think they are buying the goods or services of the well-known trader when in fact they are being duped into purchasing those of the infringer. Frequently, an infringer's goods or services are of a poorer quality. This is likely to have two effects: first, a reduction in the better-known competitor's sales; and second, harm to the better-known competitor's business reputation.

The notion of goodwill in Scots law was considered in the case of *Cruttwell* v *Lye* (1810), where the court stated that it was "nothing more than the probability that the old customers will resort to the old place". Before long, this definition was recognised as being too narrow and undeveloped. In English law the description from early on was better: in *Trego* v *Hunt* (1896), goodwill was said to be "the whole advantage, whatever it may be, of the reputation and connection of the firm". In our modern analysis of goodwill, which we looked at briefly in Chapter 1, both aspects are combined and we saw that a business's turnover of sales could be expressed in terms of a capital value. Hence, the result of passing off, which involves the filching of the better-known firm's customers and a downturn in its turnover, is quantifiable in capital terms as a loss of goodwill. The value of this capital loss – which can be substantial – may represent a good estimate of the amount of damages done to a firm by such passing-off activity.

Definition of "passing off"

"Passing off" has been defined in a number of cases of note.

In *Warnink BV* v *Townend & Sons (Hull) Ltd* (1980), Warnink, the manufacturer of the Dutch drink "Advocaat", sued the defendants for passing off as they had been selling a mixture of sherry and powdered egg under the name of "Old English Advocaat", Lord Diplock defined "passing off" as having five characteristics:

> "(1) a misrepresentation (2) made by a trader in the course of trade, (3) to prospective customers of his or ultimate customers of goods and services supplied by him, (4) which is calculated to injure the business or goodwill

of another trader (in the sense that it is a reasonably foreseeable consequence) and (5) which causes actual damage to a business or goodwill of the trader by whom the action is brought or (in a *quia timet* action [such as interdict]) will probably do so."

This definition is useful but somewhat lengthy and has been subject to some criticism.

In *Reckitt & Colman Products Ltd* v *Borden Inc (No 3)* (1990), the defendants had been selling their product in a plastic container in the shape of a lemon, but the plaintiffs had been selling lemon juice in their own container for a considerable time and their container was well known by consumers (the "Jif lemon"). Lord Oliver summarised Lord Diplock's definition into three fundamental elements (which are sometimes referred to as the "classic trinity"):

1. reputation of the plaintiff;
2. misrepresentation by the defendant; and
3. damage to goodwill.

There is no shortage of cases which illustrate these three elements.

Reputation

In every passing-off action the plaintiff must prove that it has an established reputation. Such a reputation may have been built up over a lengthy period, but the courts have had to consider the question of how long such a building-up needs to be. In *Stannard* v *Reay* (1967), a case which involved mobile fish and chip vans called "Mr Chippy", the plaintiff had built up a protectable goodwill after only 3 weeks. Nor must goodwill necessarily be built up by sales, for, in *Elida Gibbs Ltd* v *Colgate Palmolive Ltd* (1983), goodwill was built up after only a short but intensive advertising campaign. Indeed, goodwill can arise in non-commercial matters as is shown in the case of *British Diabetic Association* v *The Diabetic Society* (1996).

Business goodwill is usually built up in an area where goods and services are readily sold to consumers. Such a geographical area can be very localised or it can be global. The case of *Stannard* v *Reay* ("Mr Chippy") shows that protectable goodwill can be built up in a very localised geographical area – in that case a section of coast on the Isle of Wight. At the other extreme, in *Sheraton Corp of America* v *Sheraton Motels* (1964), the American hotel chain was able to prevent a British motel business from trading on its goodwill, claiming that the American chain had an established global goodwill since any British citizen could go into a travel agent in the UK and order a package holiday, choosing to stay in a Sheraton hotel at their destination – the global brand was recognisable by people here and so there was a likelihood of confusion on the part of the consumer.

The issue of confusion of the consumer is therefore a very important factor and in *Anheuser Busch Inc* v *Budejovicky Budvar* (1984), a case involving the American Budweiser company in one of its repeated attempts to try to prevent the original Czech Budweiser beer company from using the name "Budweiser". At the time, the American "beer" was available in the UK only in the bars of American Air Force bases and so was unknown to the British consumer. The court held that there was no likelihood of confusion. In the case of *Jian Tools for Sales Inc* v *Roderick Manhattan Group Ltd* (1995), the tool company was able to establish that it could protect its name because it had built up global goodwill from Internet sales.

Misrepresentation

It is not necessary that the misrepresentation is deliberate. As we saw in Lord Diplock's definition (above), it is only necessary that a loss of sales should arise as a reasonably foreseeable consequence. Misrepresentation can come about by any form of conduct likely to confuse the consumer.

Using the mark or name of the plaintiff's product

In *Wilkinson Sword Ltd* v *Cripps & Lee Ltd* (1982), the passing off involved both the name and the quality of the goods. The plaintiffs, Wilkinson Sword, had an established good name for selling quality razor blades. The imitation imported as "Wilkinson blades" was of inferior quality. In this case the use of the name "Wilkinson" clearly gave rise to potential for confusion, as both businesses were selling razor blades and competing for the same customers. Where there is no likelihood of confusion, a passing-off action will fail. In *Stringfellow* v *McCain Foods* (1984), the plaintiff, a well-known nightclub owner, claimed that there was passing off since the defendants had advertised their products, a thin form of oven-ready chip, under the name of "Stringfellows" and had used graphics indicating dancing chips in their advertising. The court held that there was no likelihood of confusion between the plaintiff's nightclub businesses and the oven-ready chips. The plaintiff and defendants were not competing for the same customers and the court found that the plaintiff's business had suffered no damage or loss of turnover.

Using the design or shape of the plaintiff's product or get-up

We saw that in *Reckitt & Colman Ltd* v *Borden Inc* (1990) the ("Jif lemon" case), the plaintiffs' product container, a plastic lemon, had been copied. In *The European* v *The Economist Newspapers* (1996) the court stated that in deciding whether there was a likelihood of confusion, "judicial first impression was of some importance".

Using the plaintiff's advertising theme

This could occur if, say, Lidl stores were to commence an advertising theme such as "every Lidl helps", which would trespass on the similar theme currently used by the competing Tesco stores: "Every little helps". But see below for the consequences of mere "advertising puff".

Confusion between similar-sounding product names

In *Neutrogena Corp* v *Golden Ltd* (1996), the court had to consider the use of the words "NEUTROGENA" and "NEUTRALIA" and decide whether, on a balance of probabilities, a substantial number of the public would be misled into purchasing the defendants' products.

Because, in each case, a central issue is the likelihood of public confusion between competing goods and services, it is relevant to consider customer surveys, as was shown in the case of *Imperial Group Ltd* v *Philip Morris & Co Ltd* (1982).

Damage

Even though a claimant's goodwill is often quantifiable, the extent of damage need not be tangible. It is enough to show that it is a reasonably likely result. There are a number of cases where businesses selling goods with well-known quality or origin names have been protected against potential threats:

In *Taittinger SA* v *Allbev Ltd* (1993), the champagne house was (on behalf of all the champagne producers) able to stop Babycham from being advertised as "champagne perry", even though there was no requirement in that case to show damage or loss of trade.

Similarly, in *Matthew Gloag & Sons Ltd* v *Welsh Distillers Ltd* (1998), the Scotch whisky producer was able to stop the Welsh distillers from selling "Welsh whisky". The word "whisky" is one which is exclusively descriptive of Scottish origin.

In *Consorzio del Prosciutto di Parma* v *Asda Stores Ltd* (1998), the Consorzio (co-operative) was able to stop Asda from selling its own version of "Parma ham", as its product was not sliced and packaged in Parma under supervision of a member of the Consorzio. That was regarded as a quality issue and no loss of sales required to be shown.

Injurious falsehood

In passing off, it is not necessary, as we have seen, to establish a deliberate attempt to harm the business of the plaintiff. However, where harm is intended it will be an aggravation. Such harm typically involves maliciously making false statements about the pursuer's goods or services in such a way as is calculated to cause damage. Mere "advertising puff" is not enough.

In *Ratcliffe* v *Evans* (1892), the defendant put out a newspaper advert saying that the plaintiff had died and his business had ceased. This caused the plaintiff's business to lose a huge number of customers and a great deal of turnover. The court held that this was a clear case of malicious damage.

However, in *British Airways plc* v *Ryanair Ltd* (2001), Ryanair had run an advertising campaign emphasising the high cost of its route competitors. The campaign included the phrase "EXPENSIVE BA – – – – DS!". British Airways ("BA") sued, saying that this was a malicious campaign designed to damage the reputation of its business. The court held that it was merely "advertising puff" and not motivated by maliciousness.

Domain names and cybersquatting

Cybersquatting is a form of passing off which occurs digitally. It involves individuals ("cybersquatters") registering Internet domain names indicating a connection with an established business. In *British Telecommunications plc* v *One in a Million Ltd* (1999), the defendant company had registered a large number of domain names such as "ladbrokes.com", "sainsbury.com", "marksandspencer.com", "bt.org" and a host of others. The court held that the defendants were passing themselves off as the much better known public companies and that there was therefore an attempt to take advantage of the goodwill of the better-known companies. Often, cybersquatters register such names in order to attempt to sell the domain names to the better-known companies rather than to obtain sales from those companies by fraudulent trading. But such name sale attempts are still highly objectionable. Today, it is no longer necessary to raise a passing-off action in court, as there is an alternative procedure for removing cybersquatters. It is open to an aggrieved business to request that the Internet Corporation for Assigned Names and

Numbers (ICANN) adjudicate on the matter and cancel the offending bad faith registration.

Essential Facts

- Passing off occurs when one business falsely trades upon the confusion of its goods and services with those of a well-known competitor which has an established goodwill in the market concerned and with the result that the well-known business loses sales turnover.
- In *Reckitt & Colman Products Ltd* v *Borden Inc (No 3)* (1990), Lord Oliver summarised passing off into three fundamental elements:
    - (1.) reputation of the plaintiff;
    - (2.) misrepresentation by the defendant; and
    - (3.) damage to the palintiff's goodwill.
- Reputation must have been built up, but the building-up period does not need to be a lengthy one.
- Business goodwill can be built up in a local geographical area or a global one, depending always on the established extent of the plaintiff's business.
- The issue of confusion of the consumer is therefore a very important factor. Customer surveys can be relevant to establish the extent of such confusion.
- It is not necessary that the misrepresentation is deliberate. It is necessary only that a loss of sales should arise as a reasonably foreseeable consequence.
- Misrepresentation can come about by various forms of conduct likely to confuse the consumer. For example: using the mark or name of the plaintiff's product; using the design or shape of the plaintiff's product or get-up; using the plaintiff's advertising theme; or confusion between similar-sounding product names.
- Injurious falsehood, an aggravation of passing off, is a deliberate attempt to harm the business of the plaintiff. Such harm typically involves maliciously making false statements about the pursuer's goods or services in such a way as is calculated to cause damage. Mere "advertising puff" is not enough.
- Cybersquatting is a form of passing off occurring where individuals (cybersquatters) register Internet domain names indicating a

connection with an established business. An aggrieved business can request that the Internet Corporation for Assigned Names and Numbers (ICANN) adjudicate on the matter and cancel the offending bad faith registration.

Essential Cases

Reckitt & Colman Products Ltd v Borden Inc (No 3) (1990): the defendants copied the lemon-shaped plastic container used by the plaintiffs.

Stannard v Reay (1967): this was a case involving mobile fish and chip vans called "Mr Chippy"; the plaintiff were held to have built up a protectable goodwill in a local area after only 3 weeks.

Elida Gibbs Ltd v Colgate Palmolive Ltd (1983): goodwill was built up after only a short but intensive advertising campaign.

British Diabetic Association v The Diabetic Society (1996): goodwill arose in non-commercial matters.

Sheraton Corp of America v Sheraton Motels (1964): the American hotel chain was able to show that it had an established global goodwill, since any British citizen could go into a travel agent in the UK and order a package holiday, choosing to stay in a Sheraton hotel at their destination

Anheuser Busch Inc v Budejovicky Budvar (1984): the American Budweiser company was involved in one of its repeated attempts to try to prevent the original Czech Budweiser beer company from using the name "Budweiser". At the time, the American "beer" was available in the UK only in the bars of American Air Force bases and so was unknown to the British consumer. The court held that there was no likelihood of confusion.

Jian Tools for Sales Inc v Roderick Manhattan Group Ltd (1995): the tool company was able to establish that it had built up global goodwill from Internet sales.

Wilkinson Sword Ltd v Cripps & Lee Ltd (1982): the passing off involved both the name and the quality of the goods. The imitation imported as "Wilkinson blades" was of poor quality. In this case the use of the name "Wilkinson" clearly gave rise to potential for confusion of the public, as both businesses were selling razor blades and competing for the same customers.

Stringfellow v McCain Foods (1984): the defendants had advertised their products, a thin form of oven-ready chip, under the name of "Stringfellows" and had used graphics indicating dancing chips in their advertising. The court held that there was no likelihood of confusion between the plaintiff's nightclub businesses and the oven-ready chip business. The plaintiff and defendants were not competing for the same customers and the plaintiff's business had suffered no damage or loss of turnover.

Neutrogena Corp v Golden Ltd (1996): the court had to consider the use of the words "NEUTROGENA" and "NEUTRALIA" and decide whether, on a balance of probabilities, a substantial number of members of the public would be misled into purchasing the defendants' products.

Taittinger SA v Allbev Ltd (1993): the champagne house was (on behalf of all of the champagne producers) able to stop Babycham from being advertised as "champagne perry".

Matthew Gloag & Sons Ltd v Welsh Distillers Ltd (1998): the Scotch whisky producer was able to stop the Welsh distillers from selling "Welsh whisky".

Consorzio del Prosciutto di Parma v Asda Stores Ltd (1998): the Consorzio (co-operative) was able to stop Asda from selling its own version of "Parma ham", as its product was not sliced and packaged in Parma under supervision of a member of the Consorzio.

Ratcliffe v Evans (1892): the defendant put out a newspaper advert saying that the plaintiff had died and his business had ceased. This caused the business to lose a huge number of customers and a great deal of turnover. The court held that this was a clear case of malicious damage.

British Airways plc v Ryanair Ltd (2001): Ryanair had run an advertising campaign emphasising the high cost of its competitors. The campaign included the phrase "EXPENSIVE BA – – – – DS!". British Airways ("BA") sued, saying that this was a malicious campaign designed to damage the reputation of its business. The court held that it was merely "advertising puff" and not motivated by maliciousness.

British Telecommunications plc v One in a Million Ltd (1999): the defendant company had registered a large number of domain names such as "ladbrokes.com", "sainsbury.com", "marksandspencer.com", "bt.org" and a host of others. The court held that the defendants were passing themselves off as the much better-known public companies and that there was therefore an attempt to take advantage of the goodwill of the better-known companies.

8 CONFIDENTIAL INFORMATION

Confidence and privacy

Confidence and privacy are different but related concepts.

A confidence exists where a secret is kept between the parties to the confidence. Confidential information imparted by one person to another in circumstances of confidence is protected at common law. An action may be raised to prevent a threatened disclosure or to seek damages for loss caused by such disclosure. There are many sorts of information which may be regarded as confidential. For example, trade secrets, price and commercially sensitive information, recipes for products, know-how, technological secrets, chemical formulae etc.

Privacy is the expectation that one person may not have to be subjected to scrutiny by other people. There are many facets of our lives which we regard as uniquely our own business and not that of others. We have expectations of privacy in the area of our private lives and our relationships. But there may be a public interest in the lives and activities of persons in the public eye. Specifically, the public interest may include (according to the Press Complaints Commission Code of Practice) the detection and exposure of crime, the protection of public health and safety, and the prevention of the public being misled by actions and statements made by persons and organisations. Certain social ceremonies, such as weddings, are inherently public acts. To a great extent our personal privacy is guaranteed by Art 8 of the Council of Europe's Convention on Human Rights (now protected in the UK by the Human Rights Act 1998). Article 8 protects the privacy of our private and family life, home and correspondence from arbitrary interference by a public authority. We also have certain rights to privacy regarding the retention and use of personal information held about us by others. This last protection is dealt with in Chapter 9.

Trade secrets

The common law recognises certain definite circumstances where there are protections against the leak of confidential information. The most obvious (and most litigated) of these concerns is the protection of trade secrets which are maintained in order to give the rightful owners an economic advantage over competitors.

Some companies prefer to keep their trade secrets secure rather than to rely on any other form of intellectual property protection. There may be many reasons for this. A successfully kept trade secret can give a company an advantage for a very long period of time before the secret becomes generally known. Patents, on the other hand, can only maintain an advantage for the monopoly period of 20 years (25 in the case of pharmaceutical patents). There are many examples of trade secrets. For example, Coca-Cola, Glayva whisky liqueur, Baxter's soups and sauces and Tunnocks caramel wafer biscuits are all products which are prepared using a trade recipe which is kept as a secure trade secret. The Coca-Cola recipe has remained secret since its invention in 1886. It is said that it originally contained "sugar crystals, caramel, caffeine, phosphoric acid, coca leaf, kola nut extract, lime extract, vanilla, glycerin and a secret ingredient known as 'merchandise 7X'". It has clearly been to the company's trade advantage to preserve its secret over a very lengthy period. It would not have been able to maintain its advantage had the recipe merely been patented, for it could then have been copied after the monopoly had expired.

Trade secrets occur wherever a business holds and exploits price-sensitive or commercially sensitive information. This is likely to be divulged to employees on a "need-to-know" basis in the course of employment. Most often, this merely involves the names of suppliers and customers. But a trade secret occurs wherever there is information which a business can use to gain commercial advantage over its competitors who do not hold the information. Trade secrets are therefore very broad in their scope. It is clearly of importance to ensure that employees realise what information is a trade secret and that they should not divulge such information (often, a business will require its employees to enter into express confidentiality agreements – but this may not be necessary where confidence is implied).

Prerequisites for confidence at common law

The general legal protections were best summarised in the case of *Coco* v *A N Clark (Engineering) Ltd* (1969). The plaintiff was the designer of the "Coco" moped and opened negotiations with the defendants with a view to involving them in the manufacture of the mopeds. After a number of months, negotiations broke down. The defendants then manufactured their own moped, using the plaintiff's design for some of the engine parts. The plaintiff sought an injunction to prevent the manufacture and sale of the defendants' mopeds, claiming that the discussions had been confidential and that therefore the defendants were not entitled to exploit the information they had received. The claim was refused. The court held that there was no relationship of confidence between the plaintiff and the defendants. For there to be such a relationship, three factors must be present:

1. the information must have the quality of confidence;
2. the information must have been communicated in circumstances implying an obligation of confidence; and
3. the information must have been used without authority.

The court held, on the facts of the case, that only the second requirement had been proved. For the claim to be successful, all three factors would have had to have been proved.

Another requirement is that the information concerned should not already be in the public domain or otherwise known generally. In the case of *Mustad* v *Allcock and Dosen (1928)* (1963), Dosen had been employed under an express confidence contract by a business, Thoring & Co, which had made fish hooks. Thoring & Co had developed special machinery to make the fish hooks. When the company became insolvent, Dosen was told that he owed no further duty of confidence to it and he went to work for Allcock, a competitor of Mustad. He revealed the design of the fish hook machinery to Allcock. Mustad then acquired the insolvent business of Thoring & Co, and applied for a patent for the fish hook manufacturing machinery which Thoring & Co had developed. Part of the patent application meant disclosing the nature and operation of the machinery. When Mustad discovered that Dosen had already revealed the design of the machinery to Allcock, it claimed it was entitled to an injunction on the ground that Dosen had breached the duty of confidence he now owed it (since it had acquired Thoring & Co's business). The court refused to grant the injunction, as the information which Mustad claimed was the subject of the duty of confidence had already been placed by it in the public domain when it applied for the patent. What Mustad had already disclosed to the world could no longer be the subject of a duty of confidence.

In the case of trade secrets, we have seen that this will very often cover detailed technical information such as the mechanics of an invention or a recipe for a product, as well as customer and supplier and financial information. Such secret information can be protected if it is detailed enough to enable another party to exploit it, but this does not apply if it is simply a general method or scheme held by one party. For this reason, while some of the information an employee acquires in the course of his employment will be confidential, other more general information will not. It would be quite unreasonable if the general skills and knowledge acquired in the course of employment could not be used by an employee in any new employment they may undertake. But the line between general and protected knowledge and information is not always easy to draw.

In the case of *Faccenda Chicken* v *Fowler* (1986), an employer's trade secrets were held to involve four factors:

1. the information must be such that the owner believes that the release of it would be injurious to him or advantageous to his rivals;
2. the owner must believe that the information is confidential or secret and not already in the public domain;
3. the above two (subjective) beliefs of the owner must be objectively reasonable; and
4. trade practices and usage will be taken into account in determining whether the information has the necessary quality of confidence.

Other confidential relationships

The law recognises many other categories of confidential relationship in which information is imparted confidentially by one person to another. The class of confidential relationships is not closed.

For example, the law recognises and protects personal secrets between a husband and a wife (*Argyll* v *Argyll* (1967) – an injunction prevented the disclosure of marital confidences); secrets between friends (*Stephens* v *Avery* (1988) – which involved a lesbian relationship); drawings by members of the Royal Family; state secrets (see below); the privileged relationships of professional confidentiality (confidential communications between doctors and patients, lawyers and clients, and bankers and customers); and information imparted in other circumstances implying confidence.

In the case of *Prince Albert* v *Strange* (1849), Queen Victoria and Prince Albert had a collection of private etchings some of which, without permission, had come into the possession of Strange and two others. It seems that impressions of the etchings had been taken from the original plates. The defendants wished to print a descriptive catalogue of these but were prevented from doing so. Lord Cottingham considered the issue of confidence and analysed this as arising from a number of different justifications. He said:

"the property of an author or composer of any work, whether of literature, art, or science, in such work unpublished and kept for his private use or pleasure, cannot be disputed ... the exclusive right and interest of the plaintiff in the composition or work in question being established, the plaintiff is entitled to the injunction of this court to protect him against the invasion of such right and interest by the defendant ... but this case by no means depends solely upon the question of property, for a breach of trust, confidence, or contract would of itself entitle the plaintiff to an injunction. The plaintiff's affidavits state the private character of the work of composition, and negative any licence or authority for publication ... I am bound to assume that the possession of the etchings ... has its foundation in a breach of trust, confidence or contract".

And quoting from a previous case, he continued:

"Every clerk employed in a merchant's counting house is under an implied contract he will not make public that which he learns in the execution of his duty. If the defendant has obtained copies ... it would very probably be by means of some clerk or agent of the plaintiff; and if he availed himself surreptitiously of the information which he could not have had except from a person guilty of a breach of contract in communicating it, I think he could not be permitted to avail himself of that breach of contract."

How long does the information remain confidential?

Even after confidential information is in the public domain, it does not imply that a person to whom it has previously been divulged in confidence may make use of it for their own economic gain. This feature of confidential information is sometimes called the "springboard doctrine" and was established in the case of *Terrapin Ltd* v *Builders Supply Co* (1967), where the defendants were employed by the plaintiffs to make prefabricated units for the plaintiffs' buildings. In order to do so, the defendants had to have access to the full details of the plaintiffs' designs and a confidentiality agreement was accordingly entered into. Sometime after the defendants ceased to make the units, they decided to produce their own buildings using prefabricated units very similar to those produced by the plaintiffs. Not surprisingly, the plaintiffs claimed a breach of confidence. The defendants argued that because any member of the public could, in theory, inspect the plaintiffs' buildings at any time, and that such inspection would reveal the previously secret design details, it necessarily followed that these details were in the public domain, or at least potentially in the public domain. And so, the point of the confidentiality agreement having ceased, they, like anyone else, were entitled to exploit the design. The court, however, decided that, since the original information in a highly specified form had been released to the defendants who were at the time within a relationship of confidence, it followed that even though the public might be able to make use of the design information obtaining it by inspection, a person to whom it had been disclosed within a relationship of confidence continued to be held under an obligation for a reasonable period after the relationship had ceased and could not exploit the information to the detriment of the original owner.

Another situation which arises is what happens when information which has been subject to confidentiality comes into the possession of a third party (a person who is not one of the parties to the original confidentiality agreement). Such a circumstance occurred in the case of *Morison* v *Moat* (1851). This case involved a partnership between Morison and Moat senior (father of the defendant). The partnership concerned the manufacture of "Morison's Universal Medicine", a product made using a secret recipe. Before his death, Moat senior divulged the recipe to the defendant and appointed him as his successor in the partnership. Morison did not know that the information had been divulged. Shortly thereafter, the partnership terminated. The defendant began to manufacture the medicine on his own account. Morison obtained an injunction to prevent this. Turner VC said:

> "The defendant admits that the secret was communicated to him by Thomas Moat. His allegation that he acquired a knowledge of it by acting as partner in the concern is disproved ... if he did acquire such knowledge, he did so surreptitiously ... It was clearly a breach of faith and of contract on the part of Thomas Moat to communicate the secret. The defendant derives under that breach of faith and of contract, and I think he can gain no title by it. ... It might indeed be different if the defendant was a purchaser for value of the secret without notice of any obligation affecting it."

Thus a third party, who has knowledge of the confidential nature of the information received may not profit from it, while a third party who acquires the information in good faith and for value, not knowing of its confidential nature is unlikely to be so constrained.

Remedies

The remedy for a threatened breach of confidence, or where commercial advantage is being taken of a breach of confidence will be interdict (injunction in England) or interim interdict (injunction). Evidence requires to be heard before a court may grant a full interdict. However, for an interim interdict to be granted, it is not necessary to have evidence before the court. Instead, the case will proceed on the basis of party statements which the judge will weigh up and then proceed to grant the interim order (or not) on the basis of the balance of convenience. Thus, if it appears to the judge that the balance of convenience favours the pursuer (plaintiff) then the interim order will be granted. The interim order has, of course, a limited duration and will require to be followed in time by a permanent order after evidence has been heard at a proof.

The case *Attorney General* v *Guardian Newspapers (No 2)* (1990), illustrates the effect of an injunction. The case concerned the publication of the memoirs of Peter Wright, a former MI5 agent, whose book, *Spycatcher*, was published in the United States but not before the *Sunday Times* had published an extract from the book in the UK. After publication in the US, the *Guardian* and the *Observer* newspapers published comments upon the book in their UK circulations. The case was brought by the Attorney General who sought various injunctions against further publication in the UK. The court considered that the *Sunday Times* was in breach of confidence in publishing an extract from the book prior to its publication in the US. The *Sunday Times* was held liable to account for the profits it had obtained thereby. The court refused to grant injunctions against the *Guardian* and *Observer* on the grounds that the book's contents had, through publication in the US, been disclosed globally and an injunction would therefore serve no purpose. An injunction against the *Sunday Times* further serialising the book was refused on the same grounds. An injunction was obtained against the *Sunday Times* to prevent publication of future revelations from secret service staff. Finally, the court considered that if the case had been against Peter Wright, an injunction could have been granted against his publishing the book in the UK, on the basis that he should not be allowed to profit from his own wrongdoing.

The other remedy available is damages. But, before damages can be granted, the wrongly disclosed confidential information must have been used in an unauthorised way to the detriment of the pursuer (plaintiff in England) or to the advantage of the defender (defendant). As we have seen in other chapters, both of these outcomes will be of relevance in the ascertainment of damages.

Defences

One important defence is that of public interest. The defence is, not that there has been no breach of confidence, but rather that a disclosure of confidential information is justifiable on the grounds of public interest.

An example of this is the case of *Lion Laboratories Ltd* v *Evans* (1984), where employees in the business manufacturing the "Lion Intoximeter" breath alcohol analysing devices used by the police discovered that there were certain circumstances in which the devices might operate defectively and give false readings. The employees were concerned that, if these particular defective conditions had by chance occurred, this could give rise to innocent people being falsely convicted of drink-driving offences. The company, Lion Laboratories Ltd, wanted to keep this information secret, as it might adversely affect confidence in its products, but the employees argued that they had to divulge the information to the press in the public interest and in the interests of justice. They did so and the court held that they were, in so doing, entitled to take advantage of the defence of public interest.

Essential Facts

- Confidence and privacy are different but related concepts. Confidential information imparted by one person to another in circumstances of confidence is protected at common law. The protection of confidential information depends on a number of factors, including: property rights, the idea of confidentiality and contract rights.

- Privacy is the expectation that one person may have not to be subjected to scrutiny by other people. Article 8 of the Convention on Human Rights (now protected in the UK by the Human Rights Act 1998) protects the privacy of our private and family life, home and correspondence from arbitrary interference by a public authority.

- The law recognises many categories of confidential relationship, including personal secrets between a husband and a wife; secrets between friends; drawings by members of the Royal Family; state secrets; and the privileged relationships of professional confidentiality, as well as trade secrets (which are the best known and most important).

- Trade secrets may include secret recipes, formulae and methods which give the owner an economic advantage over competitors. A business may prefer to maintain such advantages using secrecy rather than other forms of intellectual property protection, as such secrets may be maintained indefinitely, while other forms of intellectual property protection may subsist for only a limited period of time.

- To be protected, confidential information must demonstrate three factors:
    1. the information must have the quality of confidence;
    2. the information must have been communicated in circumstances implying an obligation of confidence; and
    3. the information must have been used without authority.
- Many trade practices are not secret. Trade secrets have been held to involve four additional factors:
    1. the owner believes that the release of the information would be injurious to the business or advantageous to rivals;
    2. the owner believes that the information is confidential or secret and not already in the public domain;
    3. the above two (subjective) beliefs must be objectively reasonable; and
    4. the court may consider trade practices and usage in assessing the quality of confidence.
- The "springboard doctrine" states that a person to whom confidential information had been disclosed within a relationship of confidence continues to be held under an obligation of confidence for a reasonable period after the confidential relationship has ceased and so may not exploit the information to the detriment of the original owner.
- A third party who has knowledge of the confidential nature of the information received may not profit from it, while a third party who acquires the information in good faith and for value, not knowing of its confidential nature, is unlikely to be so constrained.
- The remedy for a threatened breach of confidence, or where commercial advantage is being taken of a breach of confidence, is interdict (injunction in England) or interim interdict (injunction).
- The other remedy available is damages. But, before damages can be granted, the wrongly disclosed confidential information must have been used in an unauthorised way, to the detriment of the pursuer (plaintiff in England) or to the advantage of the defender (defendant).

- "Public interest" is an important defence to a claim of disclosure of confidential information. The defence is, not that there has been no breach of confidence, but rather that a disclosure of confidential information is justifiable on the ground of public interest.

Essential Cases

Coco v A N Clark (Engineering) Ltd (1969): for there to be a relationship of confidence, three factors must be present: the information must have the quality of confidence, the information must have been communicated in circumstances implying an obligation of confidence; and the information must have been used without authority. The court held that only the second requirement had been proved. For the claim to be successful, all three factors would have had to have been present.

Mustad v Allcock and Dosen (1928) (1963): Dosen was held to owe no duty of confidence since the "confidential" information had already been disclosed to the world by the plaintiffs. What is already in the public domain cannot be the subject of a duty of confidence.

Faccenda Chicken v Fowler (1986): an employers' trade secrets were held to involve four factors: 1. the information must be such that the owner believes that the release of it would be injurious to him or advantageous to his rivals; 2. the owner must believe that the information is confidential or secret and not already in the public domain; 3. the above two (subjective) beliefs of the owner must be objectively reasonable; and 4. trade practices and usage will be taken into account in determining whether the information has the necessary quality of confidence.

Terrapin Ltd v Builders Supply Co (1967): the defendants were employed by the plaintiffs to make prefabricated units for the plaintiffs' buildings. The defendants were told the full details of the plaintiffs' designs and a confidentiality agreement was accordingly entered into. Sometime after the defendants ceased to make the units, they decided to produce their own buildings using prefabricated units very similar to those produced by the plaintiffs. Although the relationship of confidence had ceased, and although the design details were in the public domain (at least theoretically), the defendants were held not to be entitled to profit from the information. The court held that a person to whom confidential information had been disclosed within a relationship of confidence continued to be held under an obligation for a reasonable period after the relationship had ceased and could not exploit the information to the detriment of the original owner. This is called the "springboard doctrine".

Morison v Moat (1851): this case involved a partnership between Morison and Moat senior (father of the defendant). The partnership concerned the manufacture of "Morison's Universal Medicine", a product made using a secret recipe. Before his death, Moat senior divulged the secret recipe to the defendant. Morison did not know that the information had been divulged. After the partnership dissolved, the defendant began to manufacture the medicine on his own account. Morison obtained an injunction to prevent this.

Attorney General v Guardian Newspapers (No 2) (1990): this case illustrates the effect of injunctions as remedies to disclosure of confidential information. The case concerned the publication of the memoirs of Peter Wright, a former MI5 agent, whose book, *Spycatcher*, was published in the United States but not before the *Sunday Times* had published an extract from the book in the UK. The *Sunday Times* was held liable to account for profits for unlawful publication of extracts prior to the book being published in the US. After that publication, the courts held the information was in the public domain and would not grant injunctions regarding further serialisation or comment.

Lion Laboratories Ltd v Evans (1984): employees disclosed to the press information that there were certain circumstances in which breath alcohol measuring devices might operate defectively and give false readings. They were concerned that innocent people might be falsely convicted of drink-driving offences. The court held that they were entitled to take advantage of the defence of public interest.

9 DATA PROTECTION

In many spheres of our contemporary life, not merely limited to our commercial activities, information about us is gathered and retained by government agencies, public authorities, organisations, businesses and individuals. Whenever we conduct a business transaction, such as supermarket shopping, in which we may pay for our goods using a debit or credit card or use a loyalty card, information is likely to be gathered not only about our financial dealings but also about our behaviour and preferences. This information is immensely valuable to businesses for the purposes of stock-taking and marketing. Other forms of information about us may be more sensitive still. For example, professional persons such as lawyers and doctors will hold information about us in their files (whether electronic or manual). In some cases, there will be professional rules of confidence, but in many cases we simply trust the persons to whom we impart information about us to use that information only in reasonable and appropriate ways. Often we are completely unaware that information about us is being gathered (for example, as we move about our location is transmitted by our mobile phones, or CCTV cameras will record our faces and the registration numbers of our cars). Inevitably, a vast amount of information is gathered about us for many purposes. What rights do we have to identify who holds information about us, to find out what information is held, to ensure that such information is only gathered lawfully, that it is thereafter retained and used appropriately, that it is kept secure and up to date, and that it is not shared without control over its eventual uses? It is for these reasons that the Data Protection Act 1998 (based upon the EU Directive on Data Protection 95/46/EC) was enacted.

Initially, the UK Government enacted a Data Protection Act in 1984 in response to an earlier Directive. However, within the European Union it was soon realised that there were still insufficient protections for the rights of individual privacy. The problem was getting and maintaining the right balance between the legitimate interests of organisations to hold, process and share data and the privacy rights of the individual data subjects not to have excessive amounts of data or incorrect data held, processed or transferred to their detriment. This was a Europe-wide problem answered by the EC Directive.

THE DIRECTIVE

The Directive has, by Art 1, twin objectives which at first sight appear to be incompatible. It states:

> "1 in accordance with this Directive Member States shall protect the fundamental rights and freedoms of natural persons, and in particular their rights of privacy, with respect to the processing of personal data;
>
> 2 Member States shall neither restrict nor prohibit the free flow of personal data between Member States for reasons connected with the protection afforded under paragraph 1."

In other words, providing Member States have complied with the requirements of the Directive which relate to individual subjects' rights and freedoms, there must be freedom of movement of personal data throughout the Community as is legitimately required by organisations and businesses.

Much of this careful balancing of interests is achieved by the Data Protection Principles which we look at below. Inevitably there are definitions in the 1998 Act to which we now turn.

IMPORTANT DEFINITIONS

Data

The Data Protection Act does not set out to regulate all data about individuals.

Section 1(1), which contains most of the following definitions, defines "data" as meaning any data which is processed automatically (for example, on a computer system), recorded with the intention that it will be processed automatically, is recorded as part of a "relevant filing system" or with the intention that it should form part of such a system, or is a relevant health, educational or public record (s 68).

Data which is recorded as part of a relevant filing system means any data which is not processed automatically but relates to individuals and is structured so that information about an identifiable individual can be readily obtained from it. This means a set of files or a card index arranged in a manner in which information about an individual can be easily located. So the Act extends to manual records as well as computer records. It is sometimes colourfully suggested that the test of a "relevant filing system" is that an office temp, newly introduced to the systems of an office, would be readily able to find the information about the individual from knowledge of the office filing systems (the "temp test").

It is also possible that a simple address book set out in alphabetical order is caught by the Act. If this contains name, address, telephone number and e-mail address it is at least arguable that it is a relevant filing system as it enables ease of access to information relating to an identifiable individual. But the Act was surely not intended to control such everyday systems? In practice there are exemptions for purely private and domestic purposes, but it is worth remembering how far reaching the 1998 Act's definitions extend – it is far too easy for organisations and individuals to overlook their statutory responsibilities with respect to data and the rights of the data subjects. An example of this occurred in the European Court of Justice criminal case against *Mrs Bodil Lindqvist* (2003). Mrs Lindqvist set up a web page for a parish church in the Swedish town of Alseda. She described news about the parish, parish workers and herself. When she published that one of her co-workers, whom she named, had injured her foot and was on half time on medical grounds, she was prosecuted under the Swedish data protection legislation (which also enacted the EU Directive) with processing data automatically while failing to register with the Swedish data protection authorities, processing sensitive personal data (medical data), and transferring personal data beyond the EU. The ECJ held that Mrs Lindqvist's Internet publishing was processing sensitive personal data by automatic means and that the private and domestic exemption did not apply to Internet publishing for religious purposes where the sensitive data were made accessible to an indefinite number of people across the globe. However, simply uploading the data onto a server in Sweden did not constitute transfer beyond the EU since, for such transfer to take place, an Internet user beyond the EU would require to view the data before transmission was initiated. In general terms then, "the act of referring, on an Internet page, to various persons and identifying them by name or by other means, for instance by giving their telephone number or information regarding their working conditions and hobbies, constitutes 'the processing of personal data wholly or partly by automatic means'". This general conclusion suggests that anyone who intends to keep or use personal data about others should consider whether such use might be regulated by data protection provisions.

Data controller

A "data controller" is a person who (either alone or jointly or in common with other persons) determines the purposes for which and the manner in which any personal data are, or are to be, processed. The data controller is the person whom the courts will regard as legally responsible for compliance with data protection provisions.

There may be two or more data controllers in respect of a single collection of personal data: for example, where a firm holds records of subcontractors and suppliers, the partners of the firm are jointly responsible for the data. The partners will control what information is retained and how it is to be processed, and they, as data controllers, are the persons who are legally responsible for compliance with the Act. In particular, data controllers have to notify the Information Commissioner that they are holding data, specifying the purposes for which they are doing so. Data controllers remain responsible for the processing of data held by them even if the processing is done by their employees or data processors acting under their instructions. It is the data controller's responsibility to institute procedures and guidelines which will protect that data and contain instructions ensuring the data are used only for legitimate notified purposes.

Processing

The concept of "processing", which is central to the Act, means any form of transaction involving the data or information including obtaining, recording or holding the information or data, carrying out *any* operation or set of operations upon the information or data (organising, adapting or altering the information or data, retrieving, consulting, using the information or data, disclosing, transmitting, disseminating, making available, aligning, combining, blocking, erasing, and ultimately destroying the data and information).

Data processor

A "data processor" is any person who processes data on behalf of a data controller (other than an employee of the data controller). An employee of the data controller is, of course, subject to the direct instructions of the data controller – and their act is that of the data controller. A data processor is therefore under separate duties in relation to the data – that is to say, they may not use the data for any purposes other than those contained in their instructions given by the data controller.

The definition of data processor therefore includes a person who carries out a mere administrative function such as a typist or a computer bureau.

These people do not have to notify the Information Commissioner for the purposes of the 1998 Act because the data and their processing are under the legal control of the data controller and are processed for instructed purposes only.

The definition of data processor is very broad and many types of persons may be classed as a data processor. This may include: mail-order catalogue agents, IT companies providing data input, data security services, back-up services, outsourced IT functions, disaster recovery services, data quality control services (verifying, checking and correcting data), any person engaged by a data controller to prepare reports using a data controller's database, an Internet service provider who provides a data controller with web pages, or web applications such as e-mail services, or persons engaged by a data controller to remove and destroy old computer printouts or archived files containing personal data, including secure deletion services. In each of these cases the data processor will be carrying out a limited function under the instructions and control of the data controller. A data processor does not require separately to notify the Information Commissioner because they are processing the data as and only as instructed by the data controller. It would therefore seem appropriate for a data controller to carry out a risk assessment when data is to be processed by a data processor and to take appropriate steps to ensure that the data is kept secure at all times and is processed only in accordance with instructions. In most cases this will involve written contractual obligations being undertaken by the processor regarding security and processing. The data controller will therefore continue to be legally responsible for the data, but this is not to suggest that a data processor acting on the instructions of a data controller is not subject to separate controls under the Act. Above all, the Act requires that data is kept secure while in the custody of a data processor and is not used for any purposes beyond the explicit instructions of the data controller.

Data subject

A "data subject" is an individual to whom the data relate. While the initial definition of data was very broad (and includes data of all types), the protection of the privacy of data subjects takes us to the heart of the balance of rights and duties with which the Act is primarily concerned. As we will see, data subjects have enforceable rights in relation to data about them.

Personal data

"Personal data" means data which relates to a living individual who can be identified from the data, or from that data taken together with other information in the possession of, or likely to come into the possession of, the data controller, and includes any expression of opinion about the individual and any indication of the intentions of the data controller or any other person in respect of the individual.

A name on its own may not constitute personal data until it is associated with an address or other information, such as a national insurance number, which together with the name will make it a unique reference to an individual data subject. Personal data also includes comments about an individual. We saw in the *Lindqvist* case how little information is required for data to be regarded as personal to an identifiable individual.

Recipient

A "recipient" (s 70) is any person to whom the data are disclosed, including any person (such as an employee or agent of the data controller, a data processor or an employee or agent of a data processor) to whom the data are disclosed in the course of processing the data for the data controller. A recipient is therefore a person who has certain duties owed to the data controller in relation to the security and processing of the data which comes into the recipient's hands. The term does not apply to a person to whom data is lawfully disclosed in the exercise of any power conferred by law and who therefore has no duties owed to the data controller in relation to such disclosure. One would hope that any personal data released under a power of law would be subject to protections and confidentiality conferred by the power of law concerned.

Third party

A "third party" means any person other than the data subject, the data controller, or any data processor or other persons authorised to process data for the data controller or processor, or the employees and agents of any of them. In other words, it means a person whom the data controller shares the data with or discloses the data to (for example, the sharing of data by a data controller in the form of names and addresses for the purposes of marketing).

As can be seen from the above definitions, a major aim of the 1998 is to identify a person who is legally responsible for the retention, security and processing of data. The data controller must know where the data is, into whose hands it goes, and remains legally responsible for all the processing of that data no matter where it ends up.

Sensitive personal data

Section 2 of the Act makes a distinction between "personal data" and "sensitive personal data" which is defined as being that data which gives information about a data subject's racial or ethnic origins, political opinions, religious or similar beliefs, membership of a trade union, physical or mental health or condition, sexual life, commission or alleged commission by the data subject of any offence, or information about any proceedings for any offence committed or alleged to have been committed by the data subject, and about the disposal of such proceedings or the sentence imposed in any such proceedings.

Sensitive data are treated somewhat differently from other personal data. While personal data can only be processed if one of a list of six conditions detailed in Sch 2 to the Act is present, for sensitive personal data there must also be present an additional condition from a list of ten further such conditions detailed in Sch 3. In broad brush terms, a data controller needs more than basic justifications to hold and process sensitive personal data.

THE CONTROLS OVER DATA: THE DATA PROTECTION PRINCIPLES

The Data Protection Principles are at the root of data protection law and they are specified in Part 1 of Sch 1 to the Act. Part 2 of the Schedule provides some interpretation of the Principles. The Data Protection Principles are as follows:

1 Personal data shall be processed fairly and lawfully. The conditions for the fair and lawful processing of **personal data** are contained in Sch 2 and require that one or more of the following six conditions is met: that the data subject has given his or her consent to the processing of the data; that the processing is necessary for the performance of a contract to which the data subject is a party or for taking steps at the request of the data subject with a view to entering into such a contract; that the processing is necessary to enable the data controller to comply with a legal obligation which they must fulfil; that the processing is necessary in order to protect the vital interests of the data subject; that the processing is necessary in order to fulfil certain public obligations such as for the interests of justice or to fulfil a statutory obligation; or that the processing is necessary in order to pursue the legitimate interests of the data controller or by a third party to whom the data are disclosed.

The conditions for the fair and lawful processing of **sensitive personal data** are contained in Sch 3 and are more stringent: that the data subject has given his *explicit* consent to the processing of the data; that the processing is necessary for the purposes of exercising or performing any right or obligation which is conferred or imposed by law on the data controller in connection with the employment; that the processing is necessary to protect the vital interests of the data subject or another person in a case where consent cannot be given by the data subject or the data controller cannot reasonably be expected to obtain the consent of the data subject; that the processing is carried out in the course of the legitimate activities of any body or association which exists for political, philosophical, religious or trade union purposes and which is not established or conducted for profit, or is carried out with appropriate safeguards for the rights and freedoms of the data subject, relates only to individuals who are members of the body or association concerned or have regular contact with it, and does not involve disclosure of the personal data to a third party without the consent of the data subject; that the information contained in the personal data has been made public as a result of steps deliberately taken by the data subject; that the processing is necessary for the purpose of any legal proceedings, taking legal advice or establishing, exercising or defending legal rights; that the processing is necessary for the administration of justice or acquired by law; that the processing is necessary for medical purposes and is undertaken by a health professional or another person or those who are under a duty of confidentiality which is equivalent to that of the health professional; that the processing deals with ethnic and racial matters and is necessary for the purposes of keeping under review the existence or absence of equality of opportunity or of treatment; that the processing is required in the substantial public interest (for example, in the prevention or detection of any unlawful act) or is necessary for the purposes of an insurance business; and so on.

In short, fair and lawful processing occurs where data is obtained in a justifiable manner, usually with the data subject's express or implied consent or in order to satisfy legal requirements incumbent upon the data controller. Implied consent is, however, a difficult area and in the case of *Linguaphone Institute* v *Data Protection Registrar* (1994) the issue of opt out was considered. The plaintiff used advertisements which gave the customer the ability to opt out of having their data shared with other companies. The customer had to tick a box to activate the opt out. The box was printed in minute print. The Data Protection Tribunal held that the small size of the print and wording of the opt out box did "not amount to a sufficient indication that the company intends or may wish to hold, use, or disclose that personal data provided at the time of the enquiry for the purpose of trading in personal data".

2 Personal data shall be obtained only for one or more specified and lawful purposes and shall not be further processed in any manner incompatible with that purpose or those purposes. The specified and lawful purposes are those purposes which have been disclosed in general terms to the Information Commissioner at the time of the registration of the data controller under s 16(1). Although such purposes must necessarily be expressed in general terms, an interpretation of which necessarily introduces a measure of subjective interpretation, it is a duty on data controllers to have sound, clear and legitimate purposes for collecting data and to be able to express these if called upon to do so by a data subject. Data controllers must also ensure that information which has been gathered for one purpose is not accessed and used for another independent purpose. The principle talks of "incompatible" purposes, but this is interpreted in a narrow manner.

3 Personal data shall be adequate, relevant and not excessive in relation to the purpose or purposes for which they are processed. In order to comply with this principle it is necessary for a data controller to identify the minimum amount of information that is required in order properly to fulfil their purpose – this is a question of fact in each case. If it is necessary to hold additional information about some individuals, such information should only be collected and recorded in those cases. This view was approved by the Data Protection Tribunal in the case of *Runnymede Borough Council CCRO v Data Protection Registrar* (1990). Accordingly, the data controller should consider for all data: the number of individuals about whom information is held; the nature of the personal data; the length of time it is held; the way it was obtained; the purpose for which the data is held; and the consequences for individuals of the holding, processing or erasure of the data. For these purposes it is usual for a data controller to devise appropriate audit trails, guidance and instructions for processing.

4 Personal data shall be accurate and, when necessary, kept up to date. Data are inaccurate if they are incorrect or misleading as to any matter of fact. The data controller will need to consider a number of relevant factors: details of when the data were recorded or last updated; details of all those involved with the data – employees of the data controller and any other people to whom they are disclosed; an assessment of the steps taken or to be taken to update the personal data; an assessment of how effective updating steps are; an assessment of the possible damage or distress to the data subject which may be caused by out-of-date personal data held about them.

5 Personal data processed for any purpose or purposes shall not be kept for longer than is necessary for that purpose or those purposes. To comply with this principle, data controllers will need to review their personal data regularly and to delete information which is no longer required for their purposes.

6 Personal data shall be processed in accordance with the rights of data subjects under this Act. This principle is contravened if the controller fails to supply information to the subject when a subject access request has been made, or fails to comply with notices lawfully given by the Information Commissioner under the Act. The data controller needs to know what these rights are and to create policies and controls to enable compliance with those rights.

7 Appropriate technical and organisational measures shall be taken against unauthorised or unlawful processing of personal data and against accidental loss or destruction of, or damage to, personal data. The issue in relation to this principle seems mainly to be about the meaning of the word "appropriate". A question of balance is required. The relevant matters would appear to be the state of technological developments, the cost of implementing security measures appropriate to prevent harm that might result as a result of breach of security, and of course the nature of the data to be protected must also be considered. In addition the data controller should take reasonable steps to ensure the reliability of staff having access to the personal data concerned. This raises a number of issues concerning policies for controlling access to information, policies ensuring business continuity, staff training and selection, and procedures for detecting and dealing with any breaches of security.

8 Personal data shall not be transferred to a country or territory outside the European Economic Area unless that country or territory ensures an adequate level of protection for the rights and freedoms of data subjects in relation to the processing of personal data. In all cases the data controller should consider the nature of the personal data, the origin and final destination of the information, the purposes for which it is intended the transferred data will be processed, the law in force in the country or territory in question, the international obligations of that country or territory, the relevant codes of conduct and other rules which are enforceable in that country or territory (generally or by special arrangement), and the security measures taken in respect of the data in that country or territory. The eighth principle does not apply where the data controller must make a transfer of the data in accordance with the situations laid out in Sch 4 to the 1998 Act.

OBLIGATIONS ON THE DATA CONTROLLER

A data controller is required under s 16 to notify the Information Commissioner of certain "registrable particulars" which include:

- his name and address, the name and address of any nominated representative;
- a description of the personal data being or to be processed and categories of data subject to which they relate;
- a description of the purpose or purposes of the processing;
- a description of any recipient or recipients to whom the data controller intends or may wish to disclose the data;
- the names, or a description of, any countries or territories outside the European Economic Area to which the data controller transfers, or intends to transfer, any data.

The data controller is also legally responsible for ensuring that the Data Protection Principles are complied with and therefore has to produce appropriate procedures, guidelines and instructions as are necessary to ensure compliance.

The data controller is the person who must fulfil the duties corresponding to the rights of the data subjects and in particular must respond appropriately to data subject requests and to any requirements of the Information Commissioner and Tribunal.

EXEMPTIONS IN PART IV OF THE ACT AND FOR "CORE BUSINESS ACTIVITIES"

Part IV of the Act (ss 27–39) specifies a range of exemptions which allow the processing of personal data for purposes recognised as being necessary in a democratic society.

These purposes include: national security, the prevention of crime and the purposes of taxation, the purposes of health, education and social work, the purposes of journalism, literature and art, the purposes of research history, and statistics, information made available to the public by operation of law, disclosures made for the purposes of legal proceedings, and domestic purposes. Some of these areas of exemption therefore relate to the processing of personal data by public authorities for the protection of society as a whole. Some exemptions relate to the operation by public authorities of public services and facilities. Some exemptions relate to the protection of the values and life of a civilised society and the individuals that comprise it and extend to the processing of personal data by persons and organisations which need not be public authorities or subject to state controls.

The provisions under s 32 relating to journalism, literature and art are separately defined in s 3 as the "special purposes" and it is usually thought that they express important values of freedom of speech which are specially necessary in a civilised society. It is thus reasonable in a free society to publish in the media such journalistic information about identifiable individuals as is necessary in the public interest regardless of whether the data subject's consent has been obtained (it will usually not have been). It is also felt appropriate to allow the creation and showing of works of art, literature and drama even where identifiable individuals may be the subject of such works.

Another important exempt area is the exemption for domestic purposes (to enable ordinary personal, private and family life) which we saw illustrated in the *Lindqvist* case above. There must usually be no duality of purpose.

Although not specifically mentioned in the 1998 Act, there are also exemptions which are recognised as necessary to enable core business activities. Under this category, it is reasonable to allow businesses to keep information on personnel matters such as pay, discipline, superannuation and work management. Exemptions also extend to a business's advertising, marketing and public relations and a business's accounts and similar business records. In each of these cases, the businesses must be able to show that their retention and processing of data is justifiable. Generally such exemptions would only be allowable for very small businesses as larger organisations would be expected to be registered. Exemptions also apply to non-profit organisations to enable the maintenance of their membership records and to permit communication with members.

SUBJECT RIGHTS AND FREEDOMS

The data subject has a reasonable expectation that, in respect of any registered data controller, the data held about them will be processed in such a way as complies with the Data Protection Principles.

Over and above such an expectation the data subject has the right (under s 7 of the Act) to require in writing any data controller to state if they hold personal data about the data subject, to give a description of any personal or sensitive personal data held by them about the data subject, to state the purposes for which the personal data is being processed, and to communicate that personal data to the data subject.

In addition, where such personal data is being processed in an automated system which evaluates the data and makes automated decisions about the data subject (such as creditworthiness, performance at work, conduct, etc), the data controller must state the logic involved in the automatic decision making.

Valid requests for data subject access must normally be responded to within 40 days and a fee of up to £10 may be charged. A response may be refused where an exemption from subject access provisions applies (for example, where this is necessary to safeguard national security, defence, public security, the prevention of crime, the economic interests of the state, regulatory functions, or the privacy of other data subjects).

A data subject has the right to demand that inaccurate data be rectified. Compensation is payable where the data subject has suffered damage or distress "by reason of any contravention by a data controller of any of the requirements of [the] Act" (s 13). The data controller may plead the defence that they took all reasonable steps to ensure compliance.

A data subject may appeal against a refusal to the Information Commissioner and also has right under s 42 of the Act to request the Information Commissioner to carry out an assessment of the data controller's processing to ensure that it complies with the Act.

A data subject also has certain rights to prevent direct marketing and against being subject to certain forms of automated decision making which produces significant legal effects.

THE ROLE OF THE INFORMATION COMMISSIONER

The primary function of the Information Commissioner is to disseminate information concerning the Act and compliance with it. This means the publication of an excellent set of guidelines written in plain English. The Information Commissioner is responsible for promoting good practice by data controllers and to promote the observance of the Act. In addition, the Information Commissioner must lay a report before Parliament annually.

The Information Commissioner also has wide-ranging powers of investigation aimed at determining that processing complies with the Act. These powers are exercised through information notices; special information notices; or powers of entry and inspection.

It should be noted that, under s 42, any individual who considers that he is directly affected by the processing of data may apply to the Information Commissioner for an assessment as to whether or not it is likely that processing has been or is being carried out in compliance with the Act. In carrying out an assessment, the Information Commissioner may serve an information notice where he has reasonable grounds for suspecting that the data controller has contravened or is contravening any of the principles. The notice requires the data controller to provide the Information Commissioner with information relating to the request within a specified time. The notice will also give details about appeal procedure.

Special information notices are used where processing relates to journalism, literary and artistic purposes. The particular context is that referred to in s 32 and relates to subject access, processing likely to cause damage or distress, automated decision taking or rights in relation to inaccurate data.

The Information Commissioner has rights to enter and inspect but a warrant will be required from a judge who will require to be satisfied that there are reasonable grounds for suspecting that a data controller has contravened or is contravening any of the Data Protection Principles or that an offence under the Act has been or is being committed. A warrant entitles the Information Commissioner or his officers or staff to execute the warrant and use reasonable force when necessary to enter and search the premises within seven days, to inspect, examine and operate any test respecting any data processing equipment, and to inspect and seize documents or other materials which may be evidence of an offence or contravention.

The Information Commissioner can enforce data protection law either through enforcement notices or by bringing a prosecution under the Act.

In addition, notice can be served on the data controller requiring them to take certain steps in relation to processing or indeed to refrain from processing.

THE TRIBUNAL AND APPEALS

The tribunal is the first line of appeal from notices served by the Information Commissioner or from a determination by the Information Commissioner under s 45. The tribunal may allow the appeal, substitute another notice if it considers that the Information Commissioner's notice are not in accordance with the law, rule that any discretion exercised by the Information Commissioner ought to have been exercised differently, cancel or vary notice, rule on the statement made by the Information Commissioner that compliance is required as a matter of urgency, or cancel a determination of the Information Commissioner.

Essential Facts

- **Data Protection Act 1998** (based upon the EU Directive on Data Protection 95/46/EC) was enacted to regulate the balance between individual privacy and the legitimate requirements of businesses to hold the data they need.
- The Act regulates any **personal data** (data identifying an individual) and **sensitive personal data** processed automatically or in a "relevant filing system" (a computerised or manual system that is structured so that information about an identifiable individual can be readily obtained from it).
- **"Sensitive personal data"** is data which gives information about a data subject's racial or ethnic origins, political opinions, religious or similar beliefs, membership of a trade union, physical or mental health or condition, sexual life, commission or alleged commission by the data subject of any offence, or information about any proceedings for any offence committed or alleged to have been committed by the data subject, and about the disposal of such proceedings or the sentence imposed in any such proceedings.
- The **"data controller"** is the person who (either alone or jointly or in common with other persons) determines the purposes for which and the manner in which any personal data are, or are to be, processed and is legally responsible for compliance with the Act.

- "**Processing**" involves almost any activity in relation to data including its collection, retention, arrangement, use, deletion and destruction.
- A "**data subject**" is an individual to whom the data relate.
- There are eight **Data Protection Principles** which state how data are to be controlled. They are:
    (1) Personal data shall be processed fairly and lawfully.
    (2) Personal data shall be obtained only for one or more specified and lawful purposes and shall not be further processed in any manner incompatible with that purpose or those purposes.
    (3) Personal data shall be adequate, relevant and not excessive in relation to the purpose or purposes for which they are processed.
    (4) Personal data shall be accurate and, when necessary, kept up to date.
    (5) Personal data processed for any purpose or purposes shall not be kept for longer than is necessary for that purpose or those purposes.
    (6) Personal data shall be processed in accordance with the rights of data subjects under the Act.
    (7) Appropriate technical and organisational measures shall be taken against unauthorised or unlawful processing of personal data and against accidental loss or destruction of, or damage to, personal data.
    (8) Personal data shall not be transferred to a country or territory outside the European Economic Area unless that country or territory ensures an adequate level of protection for the rights and freedoms of data subjects in relation to the processing of personal data.
- A data controller is required under s 16 to notify the Information Commissioner of certain "**registrable particulars**", which include: his name and address, the name and address of any nominated representative; a description of the personal data being or to be processed and categories of data subject to which they relate; a description of the purpose or purposes of the processing; a description of any recipient or recipients to whom the data

controller intends or may wish to disclose the data; the names, or a description of, any countries or territories outside the European Economic Area to which the data controller transfers, or intends to transfer, any data.

- Part IV of the Act (ss 27–39) specifies a range of **exemptions** which allow the processing of personal data for purposes recognised as being necessary in a democratic society. These purposes include: national security, the prevention of crime and the purposes of taxation, the purposes of health, education and social work, the purposes of journalism, literature and art, the purposes of research, history and statistics, information made available to the public by operation of law, disclosures made for the purposes of legal proceedings, and domestic purposes. Although not specifically mentioned in the 1998 Act, there are also exemptions which are recognised as necessary to enable core business activities.

- The data subject has a reasonable expectation that, in respect of any registered data controller, the data held about them will be processed in such a way as complies with the Data Protection Principles.

- The data subject has the right to require any data controller to state if they hold personal data about the data subject, to give a description of any personal or sensitive personal data held by them about the data subject, to state the purposes for which the personal data is being processed, and to communicate that personal data to the data subject. The data controller must state the logic involved in any automatic decision-making system.

- A response may be refused where an exemption from subject access provisions applies (for example, where this is necessary to safeguard national security, defence, public security, the prevention of crime, the economic interests of the state, regulatory functions, or the privacy of other data subjects).

- A data subject has the right to demand that inaccurate data be rectified. Compensation is payable where the data subject has suffered damage or distress.

- The **Information Commissioner** is responsible for maintaining the register of persons who have made notifications of their intention to process data. He is also responsible for disseminating information concerning the Act, compliance with it and good practice.

- The Information Commissioner also has wide-ranging powers of investigation aimed at determining that processing complies with the Act. These powers are exercised through information notices, special information notices, or powers of entry and inspection. An information notice requires a data controller to provide the Commissioner with information relating to the request within a specified time. Special information notices are used where processing relates to journalism, literary and artistic purposes. The Information Commissioner can enforce data protection law either through enforcement notices or by bringing a prosecution under the Act.

- The Information Commissioner may, under powers given in s 42, carry out an assessment as to whether or not processing has been, or is being, carried out in compliance with the Act.

- The **Data Protection Tribunal** hears appeals from notices served by the Commissioner or from a determination by the Commissioner under s 45.

Essential Cases

Mrs Bodil Lindqvist (2003): Mrs Lindqvist set up a web page for a parish church in the Swedish town of Alseda. She described news about the parish, parish workers and herself and reported that one of her co-workers, whom she named, had injured her foot and was on half time on medical grounds. She was prosecuted under the Swedish data protection legislation. The ECJ held that "the act of referring, on an Internet page, to various persons and identifying them by name or by other means, for instance by giving their telephone number or information regarding their working conditions and hobbies, constitutes 'the processing of personal data wholly or partly by automatic means'".

Linguaphone Institute v Data Protection Registrar (1994): the issue of opt-out was considered. The plaintiff used advertisements which gave the customer the ability to opt out of having their data shared with other companies. The customer had to tick a box to activate opt-out. The box was printed in minute print. The Tribunal held that the small size of the print and wording of the opt-out box did "not amount to a sufficient indication that the company intends or may wish to hold, use, or disclose that personal data provided a the time of the enquiry for the pupose of trading in personal data".

Runnymede Borough Council CCRO v Data Protection Registrar (1990): requiring and retaining information on dates of birth beyond what Community Charge Registration Officers were entitled to demand. Such data were held to be excessive and as such contravened the third Data Protection Principle.

10 FREEDOM OF INFORMATION

INTRODUCTION

In 1997, the UK Government first enacted some of the practical implications of "Open Government". Until then the Government's approach to official practices, documents and information was one of complete secrecy (Official Secrets Acts 1911 and 1989). Until Open Government, public employees would be liable to sign the Official Secrets Acts making it unlawful to disclose any matter of which they had acquired knowledge during their employment. In the mid-1980s, a rash of cases had been taken against former public employees who had revealed classified information which they considered had raised important public interest considerations. In many of these cases, the disclosers successfully avoided conviction (for example, Clive Ponting and Cathy Massiter). In other cases, the disclosures were made beyond the jurisdictional control of the UK courts (for example, the publication of Peter Wright's *Spycatcher* book). The Government's response at that time was to enact the 1989 Act and further to control government information. But this was to change in response to a global movement towards more Open Government in a number of democratic states.

By 1997 it was finally recognised in the UK that government secrecy was a major factor in the decline of public confidence in government and in the development of political apathy. There was also a move to increase government accountability for administrative actions. A number of other states had already implemented "Right to know" regimes without significant threats to government administration or national security.

FREEDOM OF INFORMATION ACT 2000 AND FREEDOM OF INFORMATION (SCOTLAND) ACT 2002

The UK enactment comprised two Freedom of Information Acts which were enacted in 2000 and 2002: the Freedom of Information Act 2000 (FOIA) (which sets out to create public rights to records and information held by bodies in the UK (except Scotland)) and the Freedom of Information (Scotland) Act 2002 (FOISA) (which creates public rights to records and information held by public bodies in Scotland). In both cases the information concerned is that held by government; government agencies; public authorities; public-funded bodies; and private organisations carrying out significant functions on behalf of public agencies (thus including central and local government; the Health Service (including individual GPs and dentists); publicly owned companies (eg the BBC and Channel 4 – though not in relation to journalistic materials); schools, colleges and universities; police; armed forces; other non-departmental public bodies; committees; advisory bodies; quangos; and regulators). Courts and tribunals, intelligence and security services are exempt from the Acts.

Rights to information

The general rights to require the disclosure of information are given to any "person" (individual, company or other body) (FOIA, s 1; FOISA, s 1). The Acts are intended to require a minimum of formality and as a result any written or e-mailed application for information is sufficient provided it adequately defines the applicant's name and address and clearly specifies the information requested. So, where a person makes a request by e-mail or in writing to any public authority within the jurisdiction of the respective Act, then, unless exemptions apply, that authority must:

(1) state whether it has information of the type specified in the application; and

(2) send the information to the applicant.

There is no need for an applicant to justify a request for information. "Information" means "information recorded in any form" and so includes all forms of records, electronic and manual, formal and informal, and therefore includes electronic records, tape, film, documents and others. The age of the information does not matter.

Duties on public authorities

The public authorities concerned are placed under a number of duties consistent with the need to disclose.

Generally, a public authority has 20 days in which to comply with any request, provided that it has sufficient specification to identify the information which is requested and provided also that any fees which may be due are paid (FOIA, s 10; FOISA, s 10).

While there is no requirement for the public authority to send information in any particular format, where an applicant has expressed a preference as to format, a public authority should send it in that format where this is reasonably practicable (FOIA, s 11; FOISA, s 11).

It is a criminal offence for anyone to alter, block, conceal or destroy records of information in order to prevent its disclosure once it has been requested (FOIA, s 77; FOISA, s 65), but it is not an offence for a public authority to alter or destroy records of information that have not been requested.

Public authorities are also required to have a publication scheme approved by the respective Information Commissioner, stating what information they publish or intend to publish and whether there is a charge for such publications (FOIA, s 19; FOISA, s 23). Much of this may be in accordance with codes of practice within the governmental, educational, health or other industry sector involved. The respective Information Commissioner must prepare appropriate model publications schemes (FOIA, s 20; FOISA, s 24). As a result, public authorities frequently use their Internet sites to publish information about:

- facts and analysis the Government considers important in framing major policy proposals and decisions;
- explanatory material on dealings with the public;
- reasons for administrative decisions to those affected by them;
- operational information about how public services are run, how much they cost, targets set, expected standards and results, and complaints procedures.

Public authorities are required to provide reasonable assistance to persons making or intending to make FOI applications (FOIA, s 16; FOISA, s 15).

Exemptions to duty to disclose and refusal to disclose

When a FOI application has been made, a public authority may decide that it does not wish to disclose the information or a part of it on the grounds that such disclosure is exempted. In these circumstances, the public authority must within 20 days of the receipt of the application inform the applicant that it has information of the description specified, that it is refusing to disclose the information, what grounds for exemption apply, and why it considers that those grounds apply (FOIA, s 17; FOISA, s 16). In Scotland, where a public authority does not hold the information applied for, it must state this fact expressly (FOISA, s 16).

To assist in the making of the decision whether or not to disclose information which it holds, the public authority must consider, on the one hand, whether there are relative exemptions which apply (in which case it will consider whether the public interest to withhold the information outweighs the public interest to disclose) or, on the other hand, whether there are absolute exemptions which apply (ie situations where the public interest does not need be considered) or alternatively circumstances in which there is no requirement to disclose.

Relative exemptions where public interest is relevant

Public interest to withhold or disclose must be considered in relation to:

- information intended by the public authorities for future publication;
- UK national security (other than information supplied by, or relating to, named security organisations, where the duty to consider disclosure in the public interest does not arise – see below under "Absolute exemptions");
- UK defence;
- international relations; internal relations within the UK;
- the UK economy;
- investigations and proceedings conducted by public authorities;
- law enforcement;
- audit functions carried out by the public authority over other bodies;
- formulation of government policy;
- the possibility of prejudice to the effective conduct of public affairs (except information held by the House of Commons or the House of Lords – which is absolutely exempt);
- communications with Her Majesty and communications about honours;
- health and safety;
- environmental information (which is now covered by separate regulations – the Environmental Information Regulations 2004 and the Environmental Information (Scotland) Regulations 2004);
- personal information (where there is no absolute exemption preventing disclosure);
- matters covered by legal professional privilege (for example, communications between a solicitor and a client);
- commercial interests of the public authority (for example, trade secrets, know-how, intellectual property, price-sensitive information,

information relating to negotiations and contracts between the public authority and private individuals and bodies with whom it has commercial relations).

These areas where public interest considerations occur are covered by the following sections of the Acts: FOIA, ss 22, 24, 26–31, 33, 35–40, 42 and 43; FOISA, ss 27–36 and 38–41.

"Public interest" is not an expression defined in either Act but it connotes a situation which subsists when a considerable number of persons in society or their interests are affected by the matter under consideration. As a result, "public interest" connotes situations where the accountability of public authorities for performance of services or spending of public money is the matter in issue; where the proper scrutiny of decision-making functions by the public authority is in issue; where information may be imparted to enable members of the public to participate in decisions offering them; and sometimes where information may be imparted in order to enhance public debate about matters of importance to a section of society. "Public interest" does not mean a situation where a large number of people in society may merely be curious in finding out about the matter raised.

Absolute exemptions

The grounds for absolute exemption are:

- information accessible to applicants by other means (for example through publication schemes, public registers, company files etc);
- information supplied by, or relating to, bodies dealing with security matters;
- court records;
- information covered by parliamentary privilege;
- information held by the House of Commons or House of Lords which might prejudice the effective conduct of public affairs;
- personal information (where there exists a right of "subject access" under the Data Protection Act 1998;
- information which concerns a third party and where disclosure would breach one of the Data Protection Principles);
- information provided to the public authority in confidence;
- prohibitions on disclosure under the provisions of any enactment or where disclosure would constitute contempt of court.

These areas are covered by the following sections of the Acts: FOIA, ss 21, 23, 32, 34 and 41; FOISA, ss 25, 37 and 38.

In *Common Services Agency v Scottish Information Commissioner* (2008), Mr Collie made a request for information about the occurrence of childhood leukaemia in Dumfries and Galloway, organised by year and by electoral ward. The Agency refused to give that information on the ground that because of the very low numbers of cases in the individual years and wards, it was possible for the individuals concerned to be identified and thus it had to be viewed as "personal data" which is exempt under FOISA, s 38. The Scottish Information Commissioner upheld the decision of the public authority. After appeal, the House of Lords considered that, as there was statistical technology which could allow for the proper anonymisation of low volumes of data similar to that requested, the matter should be remitted to the Information Commissioner to decide whether the information sought could be appropriately anonymised by this means and so released to Mr Collie.

Other refusals

In addition to the above exempt categories, a public authority may refuse to disclose information in three circumstances:

(1) where the cost of the provision of the information exceeds the appropriate limit (£600 in Scotland) and the public authority has decided that it will not issue a projected fee note (FOIA, s 12; FOISA, s 12);

(2) where a person makes repeated requests for the same or substantially the same information (unless a reasonable interval has elapsed); or

(3) where the request is vexatious (the request appears obsessive, harassing the public authority or distressing to its staff, designed to be disruptive or annoying, or lacks any serious purpose) (FOIA, s 14; FOISA, s 14).

Appeals to the Information Commissioners and to the courts

Public authorities' compliance with the provisions of the Acts is a matter under the respective jurisdictions of the Information Commissioner and the Information Commissioner for Scotland. Where a party claims that he has a public interest to obtain information and has been denied this information, then the aggrieved party may appeal to the relevant Information Commissioner. The Information Commissioner will issue a decision and has powers to challenge authorities who refuse to release records and may make orders requiring disclosure of information in the form of notices and enforcement notices. Third parties about whom public authorities hold information may appeal to the Commissioner on the basis that a proposed release of information about them would breach their personal privacy or commercial confidentiality or when the information was provided to the public authority in circumstances of confidentiality. In certain circumstances applicants and third parties may appeal from a decision of the Information Commissioners to the Freedom of Information Tribunal and to the courts. The procedures applying as between Scotland and the UK differ widely at this point. The case of *Sugar* v *British Broadcasting Corporation* (2009), is an example of how a case relating to the jurisdiction of the Information Commission was subject to forms of appeal and judicial review which finally reached the House of Lords on appeal.

Costs of disclosure

The provision of requested information is a service to which public authorities, after the inception of the Acts, are committed. Such provision of information involves direct and indirect costs mainly in connection with administration, searching and communication or publishing of information. In general, public authorities will absorb the costs of complying with the FOIA and FOISA. However, in some cases, the costs of providing the requested information may be above limits fixed in regulations. In these circumstances, a public authority will require to estimate the projected costs involved in answering the request and may decide to charge a fee for the disclosure (FOIA, ss 9 and 13; FOISA, ss 9 and 13). At present, under the Scottish regulations, the public authority will calculate its costs at £15 per hour for each employee utilised. If the cost are below £100, no fee will be charged. Where the projected costs exceed £100 and are below £600, the authority may charge the applicant a fee calculated as 10 per cent of the amount by which the projected costs exceed £100. If the projected costs exceed £600, then the fee is £50 for the first £600 of projected costs plus the amount by which the projected costs exceed £600 (Freedom of Information (Fees for Required Disclosure) (Scotland) Regulations 2004 and Freedom of Information (Fees for Disclosure under Section 13) (Scotland) Regulations 2004). The rates differ as between Scotland and elsewhere in the UK.

Where a fee is to be charged, the public authority must send out a fee notice to the applicant within 20 days from the date of receipt of the original request. The public authority is not required to send any information in answer to the request until any such fee has been paid.

Public records and the "30-year rule"

At present, the Public Records Office has a "30-year rule" which states that certain sensitive historical records become disclosable only after the passage of a period of 30 years (Public Records Act 1958 and Public Records Act (Northern Ireland) 1923). The FOIA (s 63*ff*) abolishes the 30-year rule and both FOIA and FOISA contain provisions which provide more discretion in the disclosing of historical public records. In most cases, earlier release will be possible, but in some cases later release may be provided for when there is good reason for continuing restriction, such as where there is a continuing political or security sensitivity or a likelihood of a substantial public harm occurring upon earlier disclosure.

Essential Facts

- The Freedom of Information Act 2000 and the Freedom of Information (Scotland) Act 2002 create public rights to require the disclosure of records and information held by public bodies in the United Kingdom and Scotland respectively.
- A "public authority" is any organisation of central and local government or other public agency, including publicly owned companies, publicly funded bodies, regulators, committees, advisory bodies, schools, colleges, universities, police, armed forces and others. The Acts do not extend to courts and tribunals.
- Any person can make a Freedom of Information application, provided that they specify their name, address and the information that they seek.
- A public authority is required to disclose any relevant specified information and records within 20 days unless that information is exempt from disclosure.
- Exemptions apply where applications are vexatious or repeated; would cost more than £600 to supply; where the information is otherwise available; where the information is covered by Data Protection disclosures or Environmental Information disclosures;

where disclosure of the information is prohibited or would amount to contempt of court; where the information is personal data, commercially sensitive data, confidential or privileged data; where the information relates to or is supplied by securities services; and, except where there is a public interest in disclosing the information, the information relates to UK national security, defence, international or internal relations, the economy, investigations, proceedings and audits of or by the public authority, government policy, and certain communications, among others – all as specified in the Acts.

- It is a criminal offence to alter, block, conceal or destroy records and information in order to prevent its disclosure once it has been requested.

- A public authority must have a publication scheme approved by the Information Commissioner who must prepare model publication schemes and codes of practice.

- Public authorities are under a duty to assist applicants to obtain the information they require and where possible in the format that they request.

- A public authority can require a contribution of the costs of disclosing the information in accordance with regulations.

- An applicant or a person affected by an application can appeal to the Information Commissioner concerned and from there further rights of appeal exist to the Freedom of Information Tribunal or to the courts.

- The Freedom of Information Acts repeal the "30-year rule" in relation to public records and provides discretion as to disclosure of such records.

Essential Cases

Common Services Agency v Scottish Information Commissioner (2008): the Agency refused to disclose details about the occurrence of childhood leukaemia organised by year and by electoral ward, on the basis that because of the very low numbers of cases in the individual years and wards, it was possible for the children concerned to be identified and thus the information had to be viewed as "personal data" which is exempt under FOISA, s 38. The House of Lords remitted the matter to the Information Commissioner so that the information could be anonymised appropriately.

Sugar v British Broadcasting Corporation (2009): the jurisdiction of the Information Commissioner was considered in various appeals and judicial reviews.

11 E-COMMERCE

WHAT IS E-COMMERCE?

Prior to the 19th century, the paradigm for buying and selling goods was face-to-face: the buyer would look at the goods in question, negotiate a price, pay the price and take delivery of the goods. For most people, if they wanted to buy things, they would have to travel to the shops or markets, or possibly salesmen might go round houses and try to persuade the occupiers to make a purchase. In all of these cases the consumer had direct, face-to-face negotiations with the seller and could examine and therefore satisfy themselves of the quality and nature of the goods before the purchase. Payment would be achieved by handing over cash or writing out a cheque. If goods were found to be faulty, or if the goods failed to be of merchantable quality, then they could be returned to the seller for repair or replacement.

From the 19th century onwards, there developed alternative ways of doing business that did not physically involve face-to-face dealings. Business could be carried out at a distance. A consumer might see an advertisement in a newspaper or on television, or respond to advertising sent through the post. This enabled a consumer to order by letter, enclosing a cheque or postal order as payment. Later still, the telephone extended ways in which business could be carried out at a distance, as people could order by phone (which really only became easy when credit cards emerged as a form of payment).

In each of these "distance selling" examples, three problem situations arose regularly:

(1) problems with a mismatch between the description of the goods and the actual quality and nature of the goods (they could not be examined before delivery);

(2) problems with payment (money could not be sent safely by post – but cheques, postal orders and credit cards have, to a great extent, solved this problem); and

(3) how can complaints about the goods be resolved?

Distance selling therefore required that special laws be developed so that consumers had statutory guarantees that advertised goods conformed to their advertised description and would be of merchantable quality. If either of these conditions was not met, the consumer could send them back. These guarantees were provided by the Trade Descriptions Act 1968 (which created the offences of applying a false description; supplying goods under a false description; or making false statements about the prices of goods or the supply of services, accommodation or facilities) and the Sale of Goods Act 1979 (as updated by the Supply of Goods and Services Act 1982, the Sale and Supply of Goods Act 1994, and the Sale and Supply of Goods to Consumers Regulations 2002). The 1979 Act was directed at resolving issues when purchases go wrong. It provides that goods must fit their description; be of merchantable and satisfactory quality; and be fit for the purposes for which they were sold. If the goods fail to meet these standards then the seller is under a statutory duty to put matters right. A customer can reject and return faulty goods within a reasonable time and obtain a refund. If a repair is offered then such repair must not overly inconvenience the purchaser.

Finally, the Consumer Credit Act 1974 (as amended, most recently, by the Consumer Credit Act 2006) has given the consumer certain protections where they purchase goods on credit, by hire purchase or by credit card payment. These include rights to full information about the terms of any credit made available; a right to a cooling-off period within which the consumer can change their mind; some rights to refunds at the expense of the merchant and credit provider (for example s 75 of the Act provides that credit card providers share a joint and several liability with merchants for consumer claims of breach of contract or misrepresentation for contracts between £100 and £30,000); and some protection against fraud. All persons who offer such credit require to be licensed and are subject to a regulatory regime.

In addition, there exist rules to enable consumers to be protected from demands for payment being made in relation to unsolicited goods (Unsolicited Goods and Services Act 1971 (as amended)).

While distance selling contracts were often created by means of a written offer and acceptance – usually in the form of a letter or coupon – the use of the telephone and credit card payment caused problems concerning how to prove whether a contract had in fact been agreed and what its terms were. Initially, much was inferred from parties' actings. With the advent of the computer age and the development of the global market using the Internet, the differences between traditional face-to-face commerce and digital commerce at a distance were particularly strongly felt. A number of problem areas were identified and these required European (if not global) solutions. At around the same time, the Data Protection Acts introduced the idea that a consumer had rights in relation to the retention and use of their personal data collected by distance retailers.

PROBLEMS INHERENT WITHIN E-COMMERCE

The problems with distance selling in a global virtual market can be summarised under a number of headings:

1. *Identity*: the purchaser and the seller want to be assured of the other's identity. When they enter into contracts, they want to know that they can identify the other party in order that they can enforce obligations if necessary. They need to know that any communication has originated with the other and has not been tampered with.

2. *Seller's reputation*: the ways in which a potential purchaser can learn from other customers about the seller's reputation are limited.

3. *Quality and value of goods*: there is no opportunity to examine the goods prior to delivery of them. What if the goods are not of reasonable quality? The purchaser needs to be able to rely on advertised information and there needs to be a satisfactory regulatory regime for obtaining redress, refund or repair if the goods fail to be of an appropriate quality or are not worth what was paid.

4. *Negotiations and contracts*: the purchaser needs to be able to receive a reasonable response from the seller when information is requested. Feedback must be of a sufficient quantity and quality and must be given within a reasonable time. Also, where digital contracts are entered into, the parties must be able to rely on the integrity of the terms they have agreed and know that the contracts are documents recognised by the courts and are enforceable.

5. *Jurisdiction*: because the parties might live in difference legal jurisdictions with very different legal assumptions, and because their communications might pass through various legal jurisdictions, the parties must know in which legal jurisdiction they can have their disputes resolved and which system of legal rules will be enforced.

6. *Payment*: payment systems must be secure from intrusion and private and effective in passing monetary value from the one party to the other (and back, where refunds are necessary).

7. *Delivery*: the purchaser must be aware of when and how the goods will be delivered. They must know what they can do to obtain

redress if there is delay in delivery or if the goods are damaged or perish in transit.

The solutions to some of these problems are primarily technical, while with others the solutions are primarily legal.

ASYMMETRIC ENCRYPTION TECHNOLOGY

With the advent of e-mail communications came the first issues about online privacy. When an e-mail message is sent it is first of all disassembled into electronic "packets" which are then sent individually along the chain of computers between the sender and the recipient. The process of sending involves copying the packets from one computer onto the next many, many times. There was therefore the possibility that a third party could capture and re-assemble the whole message. Having done so, the third party would then know its contents and would be able to change the details in the message before sending it on. Doing business negotiations by e-mail therefore encountered problems (1) and (4) above.

The solution to the problems is primarily technical and involves encryption. The e-mail requires to be encrypted by the sender and decrypted by the recipient. Traditional forms of encryption involved the sharing of a password between the sender and recipient, but the password itself was liable to being intercepted and rendered the whole exercise fruitless.

Then, in the early 1970s, mathematicians working for GCHQ in the UK discovered a method of encryption using key pairs. The first IT industry standard was produced in 1977 by three researchers at MIT in the USA, named Rivest, Shamir and Adleman, and has since become known as "RSA encryption". It is the basis of all current secure encryption systems used in e-commerce.

The technology works by each party producing a key pair, one of each being a public key and the other a private key. Both keys are necessary in order to complete the cycle of encryption and decryption of the message. The parties share their public keys but keep their private keys to themselves. When the sender wishes to send an encrypted message, they encrypt the message using their private key *and* the recipient's public key. The recipient is able to decrypt the message using their private key and the sender's public key. A third party will be able to access only the parties' public keys and so will not have all the keys necessary to decrypt the message or tamper with it.

Asymmetric encryption and decryption technology therefore allows e-mails and other documents to be created and communicated between the parties privately and without any risk of interception or tampering. The technology satisfies the requirements of allowing the recipient to identify the sender uniquely (since only the sender will have the private key needed to encrypt the message which the recipient can decrypt using the sender's public key): this feature is known as "authenticity". The technology also guarantees the privacy and "integrity" of the message (since only the recipient can decrypt the message, he knows that no third party has been able to tamper with it).

While the asymmetric key encryption technology appears, at first sight, to be somewhat cumbersome (since there must be the sending of the public keys and the encrypting of messages), in fact this is all now carried out using encryption applications and the parties will usually not be aware that their communications are encrypted at all. For example, Amazon's "shopping basket" technology uses an asymmetric key encryption system known as SSL (secure socket layer) technology and the only indication that the user has of this is that the URL starts with "https://" rather than "http://"). To a great extent, problems (1) and (4) above are resolved by this technology.

DIGITAL SIGNATURES

Technology was not enough to create confidence in the use of encryption for secure and private electronic communications. Therefore the EU adopted asymmetric key encryption technologies when it issued the Directive on a Community framework for electronic signatures (99/93/EC) which was enacted in the UK by the Electronic Communications Act 2000 and followed by the Electronic Signatures Regulations 2002 (SI 2002/318).

The 2000 Act lays out the need for a system of reliable and secure encryption technologies to be provided and creates (by ss 1–6) an approval scheme whereby persons or organisations who provide encryption services can be registered. Some of these, who hold encryption keys for clients, are referred to as "Trusted Third Parties". The aim is stated to be to create public confidence in such providers and to reduce the incidence of fraud. Section 7 allows digital signatures, supporting encryption certificates and encryption processes to be admitted as evidence in court and gives the courts the power to decide whether signatures are genuine, have been properly used and what weight they should carry. In this way, the technical and legal requirements of electronic contracting have been placed on a sure footing across the European Economic Area.

Therefore, in practice, the solutions to problems (1) and (4) above are provided primarily by technological developments, and technology remains the driving force in the development of solutions to these and a number of other of the problems inherent in e-commerce, but the courts may now, by virtue of additional legislative developments, recognise, take into account and enforce contracts negotiated, drawn up and communicated entirely electronically.

E-COMMERCE AND THE LEGAL REQUIREMENT AS TO FORM

Traditionally, a contract may be made in a number of different forms. For example, contracts may be made by deed; made in writing; evidenced in writing; oral; deemed from the actings of the parties; or made by a combination of these methods.

Sometimes the requirements as to form are set down by statute. The Sale of Goods Act 1979 states that a contract of sale "may be made in writing (either with or without seal), or by word of mouth, or partly in writing and partly by word of mouth, or a may be implied from the conduct of the parties".

Clearly, a sale of goods and services contract allows some flexibility in its form – but there are certain types of contract (such as those for heritable property) which require to be committed to writing. Nonetheless it would be very foolish to enter into a contract for the purchase or sale of goods of substantial value unless the precise terms were negotiated and committed to writing, if only to provide appropriate evidence necessary for an action for enforcement, implement or damages. It remains the case that the more important commercial contracts still require to be expressed in writing, for example an assignment of copyright or other intellectual property rights, a consumer credit agreement, certain mercantile documents, and so on.

The Interpretation Act 1978, Sch 1, defines "writing" to include "typing, printing, lithography, photography and other modes of representing or reproducing words in a visible form, and expressions referring to writing are construed accordingly". It has been suggested that this definition is already wide enough to include words stored in computer data form which may be reproduced on screen or printed on paper as a document. It therefore appears that, provided we can be satisfied that a contract constituted by e-mail offer and acceptance can be relied upon as sufficient evidence of the contents, then such a contract would appear to be perfectly valid as a medium expressing agreement for the purchase of goods and services of substantial value.

It was the advent of e-mail and web commerce that brought about the start of a new category of business called "e-commerce". Such business is driven by global rather than local market forces. There is no doubt that web commerce has the competitive edge: retailers can sell goods globally and so are not restricted to their geographical locality. In addition, retailers don't need to have retail premises or shop assistants in the customers' localities – a single warehouse will do; nor is there a need for the distribution systems and costs which are involved in distribution to local retail centres. For the first time, a consumer surfing the net for shopping is just as likely to encounter a distance seller in the UK as they are to encounter one elsewhere in Europe, or indeed in America or Asia. It is this global nature of e-commerce which has produced problems. A number of issues became prominent and required standard solutions. For example: what jurisdiction governs an e-commerce contract? How can a contract be created purely electronically? How can such a contract be proved? How can the consumer's rights on sale be protected? Can rules be made to ensure that goods conform to their virtual description? What rights does the consumer have to return or reject goods? How do we protect the consumer's personal data from being misused? Can control be placed upon the ever-increasing volumes of spam advertising e-mail? How are payment systems to be controlled and protected from fraud? How is the consumer, and indeed the distance seller, to be protected from fraud? How do we know when a contract has been concluded virtually? What evidence do we have of the creation of a contract? How does a consumer delete or amend data entered in error? It became clear that a trans-European regime was required which would resolve these issues.

But, at the same time, it can be seen that most of these issues are not new questions: it is simply that the amount of business now being conducted on the Web requires that a strong regulatory framework is developed for this new form of virtual communication. The European Union, standing that its purposes include the free passage of goods and services, was in a good position to harmonise laws. The first stage of this harmonisation was the consumer's rights and protections and marketing issues which were dealt with in the Distance Selling Directive (which is, of course, relevant just as much to telephone sales as to Internet sales). The second stage dealt with other technical concerns mainly related to the creating, signing and proving of electronic contracts and with issues of security and confidentiality of communications. Equally, there are commercially driven global movements which are involved and a number of solutions which came to be used for some of these problems are technical rather than legal – this is particularly so with payment systems and security and confidentiality issues.

E-COMMERCE DIRECTIVE

The EU E-commerce Directive (Directive 2000/31/EC) was intended to create a unified system for the regulation of "contracts concluded by electronic means". Member States must ensure that the legal requirements applicable to the contractual processes neither create obstacles for the use of electronic contracts nor result in such contracts being deprived of legal effectiveness and validity on account of their having been made by purely electronic means.

When a contract is concluded between a business and a consumer via a website (but not when it is concluded between businesses, or where the parties have otherwise agreed, or where the contract is concluded wholly by e-mail), the "service provider" (an e-commerce merchant) must provide certain information.

Article 5 of the Directive states that required information includes the name, address and reliable contact details of the service provider and whether the service provider is on a trade or other public register and subject to an authorisation scheme or under a supervisory regime.

Article 9 requires Member States to remove any prohibitions or restrictions on the use of electronic contracts. Exceptions may be made in the following areas:

- contracts that create or transfer rights in real estate, except for rental rights;
- contracts requiring by law the involvement of courts, public authorities or professions exercising public authority;
- contracts of suretyship granted and on collateral securities furnished by persons acting for purposes outside their trade, business or profession;
- contracts governed by family law or by the law of succession.

Article 10 provides that, in respect of consumer contracts, service providers must provide consumers with at least the following information, prior to the order being placed by the recipient of the service:

- the different technical steps to follow to conclude the contract;
- whether or not the concluded contract will be filed by the service provider and whether it will be accessible;

- the technical means for identifying and correcting input errors prior to the placing of the order;
- the languages offered for the conclusion of the contract.

Furthermore, service providers must indicate to consumers any relevant codes of conduct to which they subscribe and information on how those codes can be consulted electronically. Contract terms and general conditions must also be provided to the recipient in a way that allows him to store and reproduce them.

Article 11 states that when consumers of services place their orders through technological means, the service provider has to acknowledge the receipt of the recipient's order without undue delay and by electronic means. The order and the acknowledgement of receipt are deemed to be received when the parties to whom they are addressed are able to access them.

Recitals 34–39

The spirit of the Directive in respect of online contracts is expressed in Recitals 34–39 which in essence provide that each Member State must amend its legislation containing requirements, and in particular requirements as to form, which are likely to curb the use of contracts by electronic means. The result of such amendments should be to make contracts concluded electronically workable. However, the Directive does not affect Member States' possibility of maintaining or establishing general or specific legal requirements for contracts which can be fulfilled by electronic means, in particular requirements concerning secure electronic signatures.

Moreover, Member States may maintain restrictions for the use of electronic contracts with regard to contracts requiring by law the involvement of courts, public authorities, or professions exercising public authority; this possibility also covers contracts which require the involvement of courts, public authorities, or professions exercising public authority in order to have an effect with regard to third parties as well as contracts requiring by law certification or attestation by a notary.

DISTANCE SELLING DIRECTIVE

E-commerce takes up the concepts of distance selling which first became commonplace when people received and ordered from catalogues. The problem of distance selling was not created by computer technology. Traditional forms of commerce did latterly include the distance selling of goods and services, with some forms of distance payment methods becoming common.

With the advent of the Internet, bringing with it a host of new jurisdictional problems, the problems became more crucially felt and it became clear that distance selling also needed to be placed on a sure footing across the European Economic Area. This was provided in the Distance Selling Directive (Directive 97/7/EC).

Article 2 defines a "distance contract" as: "any contract concerning goods or services concluded between a supplier and a consumer under an organised distance sales or service provision scheme run by the supplier, who, for the purpose of the contract, makes exclusive use of one or more means of distance communication up to and including the moment at which the contract is concluded". "Distance communication" includes "any means which, without the simultaneous physical presence of the supplier and the consumer, may be used for the conclusion of a contract between those parties". There is an indicative list (Annex I) which includes offers by letter, printed matter, press advertising, catalogues, television, radio, telephone and fax contracts as well as e-mail and Internet contracts.

Article 4 requires the distance selling merchant to provide the following information:

- the identity of the supplier and, in the case of contracts requiring payment in advance, his address;
- the main characteristics of the goods or services;
- the price of the goods or services including all taxes;
- delivery costs, where appropriate;
- the arrangements for payment, delivery or performance;
- the existence of a right of withdrawal;
- the cost of using the means of distance communication, where it is calculated other than at the basic rate; and
- the period for which the offer or the price remains valid.

Article 5 states that the merchant must provide written confirmation of the contract (this has been interpreted by the Department of Trade and Industry to include e-mail confirmation). Article 6 gives the consumer certain rights of withdrawal. Article 8 deals with credit card payment and requires Member States to ensure that their law provides a cooling-off period for cancellation and protections which allow a consumer to be recredited with their money in the event of a fraudulent transaction.

Article 9 prohibits "inertia selling" whereby unsolicited goods and services are followed up with a demand for payment.

As a measure against the annoyance of "cold calling" and similar practices, Art 4 provides that "in the case of telephone communications, the identity of the supplier and the commercial purpose of the call shall be made explicitly clear at the beginning of any conversation with the consumer". Article 10 provides that automated telephone calling systems and fax machines may be used only with the prior consent of the consumer. An automated calling system is a computer-controlled system which dials telephone numbers and, when these are answered, plays a pre-recorded message to the recipient. These are unlawful in the United Kingdom without obtaining a licence from Oftel.

WHEN AND WHERE IS THE CONTRACT MADE?

As we will see with cybercrime, it is important that we should know the jurisdiction within which a particular juridical act is conducted. Most contracts will contain a term, often at the end of the agreement, stating which country's laws should be used to interpret and enforce the contract. Since contracts may now be completed between persons situated in different countries, it is important that, at least for the purposes of electronic contracts, there is some global agreement of material terms and of phrases.

On occasions, the contract is silent as to the applicable law, but appropriate and pragmatic rules have been developed in the courts to determine which jurisdiction applies. The basic rule is that the applicable law is that of the country in which the contract is made. This worked well where parties both reside within one jurisdiction or where the contract is signed within one jurisdiction, but the problem is obviously more difficult when parties reside in different jurisdictions. It is important to realise that there is nothing new about this situation – the same problems occur where parties in different countries enter into written contracts with each other. But it is much more common to encounter this problem today. In the past, a set of rules was created to allow jurisdiction to countries in which a contract was physically made (because both parties were present at its signing) or where the contract was to be performed. And in relation to enforcement, courts have traditionally taken the view that they have jurisdiction where a defendant is resident within their geographic jurisdictional area. The questions, at least of place of making (signing) and performance, do not readily transfer to electronic commerce.

The only acceptable solution at present is to ensure that there is always a clause identifying the supervising jurisdiction.

The issue of when the contract is made is a simpler problem since Scotland (in common with England and common law legal systems) has a "postal rule" to interpret difficulties arising out of the making of an offer and of its acceptance and the role of the delivery medium. The contract is concluded as soon as there is *consensus in idem* between the seller and the purchaser and both parties have actual or constructive knowledge of this. Of course, with e-mail, the speed of the transaction would remove many of the problems which have occurred in relation to the delivery medium.

An interesting academic problem occurs where automatic technology, used by web-based vendors, is used to make contracts with consumers. In these cases, there is, strictly, no human mind involved in the conclusion of the contract. But it cannot be argued that there is no *consensus in idem* since the automatic processes are rule governed and the rules embody a human-created policy whereby the vendor commits itself to contracting in the event that a consumer inputs identity, offer and payment data which satisfies the rules. *Consensus in idem* is therefore indirectly involved when, and only when, the policy is satisfied.

"BEST EVIDENCE" AND HEARSAY

As we have seen, the Electronic Communications Act 2000 acknowledges the admissibility of electronic signature and integrity verification of documents in court proceedings. Recent changes in civil evidence have also acted to diminish the force of the hearsay rule – this means that in principle, unless there exist good reasons for not doing so, evidence of electronic contracts will be admitted in civil proceedings even if this evidence is in the form of computer print-outs and computer-generated documents. However, there may be good reasons for a party to such proceedings to require the party relying on such evidence to lead evidence in support of such documents and to show how the print-outs and documents are generated from the stored data, how that stored data was initially input into the computer system, how the structure of rules, procedures and other automatic systems used in a computer application has given rise to the contract and output reports, and whether an audit of the operation of these rules, procedures and systems shows that they are applied consistently or otherwise. That is to say, the computer system and program, if challenged, have to be properly set up in court. These factors will clearly have a bearing upon the weight which the court gives to the computer-generated evidence which is produced before it.

In criminal proceedings, the hearsay rule subsists and there is no prospect of replacing it. But, even so, there are now procedures authorised by Act of Adjournal which allow the admission of routine evidence and of computer evidence but provide for the possibility of challenging of such evidence. In the event that the evidence is challenged, it then becomes necessary for parties to support the evidence by using the criteria above mentioned.

The force of the "best evidence" rule is that only the most direct evidence of any fact under consideration by the court should be received and relied upon. Any prejudice to a contesting party must be eliminated. It has been suggested that the best evidence of matters evidenced on a computer print-out is the evidence of the persons who input the data in the first place or who developed the program that uses the data. To all practical purposes, in civil proceedings the "best evidence" rule has, like the hearsay rule upon which it is based, disappeared. But in civil proceedings the weight of the evidence may be assessable only after evidence has been led as to how the computer-generated evidence has arisen out of the input data and programming. In criminal proceedings it remains the case, despite the Act of Adjournal, that both admissibility and weight of computer-generated evidence depend on whether a challenge is made and, if so, the outcome of the evidence supporting or contesting the evidence.

CONCLUSION

Given that electronic commerce is a relatively new phenomenon which has grown enormously over the last 8 or 9 years, it is surprising how quickly the European Union has prepared detailed Directives to provide for its regulation. These have provided a system for harmonising e-commerce and creating conditions for its development but at the same time have balanced the needs of individuals for privacy. The Directives, while quickly providing the basis for the achievement of e-commerce, have perhaps two faults: first, that they have been prepared without a full analysis of the inherent problems involved and without consideration of the consequences; and, second, that, on a global level, many of these problems will probably be answered finally with technological solutions rather than with legal ones. For example, the legal issues concerning encryption key-holders are perhaps unnecessary ones, since in most cases consumers are quite happy to conduct business over SSL secure websites without considering whether the websites concerned are appropriately verified by UK or EU Trusted Third Parties. Nor does it appear that in most instances the jurisdictional problems which could occur are a disincentive to much web-based business. In the final analysis, the interlay between technological and legal controls make this an interesting and challenging area of commerce which is likely to evolve considerably over the coming 10 years – however, the legal foundations have now been laid, and it is perhaps only fine tuning which still requires to be established.

Essential Facts

- E-commerce involves buying and selling goods over the Internet and therefore can involve suppliers and customers in distant legal jurisdictions. Traditional face-to-face paradigms are rendered inappropriate. A number of specific difficulties are encountered: buyer and seller need to know the other's identity and trust their reputation; the buyer must be satisfied of the quality and value of goods; there needs to be a mechanism for entering into binding contracts; there need to be systems for the payment of goods and of redress for defective goods; and both parties should know how and in what legal jurisdiction to resolve any disputes. Some of these problems had already arisen in connection with catalogue and telephone sales. In the European Economic Area, harmonised solutions were provided by the issue of Directives on distance selling and e-commerce and by the development of encryption technologies.

- Encryption (the use of asymmetric pairs of public and private keys to encode e-mail and other transactional steps) provides a technical means for enabling secure and private communication between a buyer and a seller. Communications have "integrity" (they cannot be interfered with or changed by third parties) and "authenticity" (the parties are able to satisfy themselves that the communications originate from the other). Legal provisions (the Directive 99/93/EC on a Community framework for electronic signatures, which was enacted in the UK by the Electronic Communications Act 2000 and followed by the Electronic Signatures Regulations 2002 (SI 2002/318)) establish a system of trusted encryption services and enable legally enforceable documents to be signed with a "digital signature" recognised by the courts.

- Articles 9, 10, 11 and Recitals 34–39 of the EU E-commerce Directive (Directive 2000/31/EC) allow contracts to be concluded by electronic means, including by e-mail or using websites. The e-merchant has to provide their name, geographical address and reliable contact details. The full terms and conditions of the contract, and the existence of any relevant codes of conduct, must be disclosed in such a way that they can be recorded. Customers must be provided with a means of identifying and correcting input errors before the final conclusion of the contract. Customer privacy is maintained.

- Distance Selling Directive (Directive 97/7/EC) is aimed at creating consumer confidence in non face-to-face contracts. This includes a wide range of forms of distance contract as well as Internet and e-mail contracts. Article 4 states the prior essential information which the supplier must provide to a purchaser. Once a contract is formed, written confirmation must be provided by the supplier. The consumer has rights of withdrawal and a cooling-off period where payment is by credit card. Protections are given against fraud when payment is made by card. Inertia selling of unsolicited goods and services is prohibited. Restrictions are placed on "cold calling" and automated calling systems.

12 CYBERCRIME

Criminals started to devise ways of using information technology to carry out their illicit purposes from the first time that automated electronic devices became connected over networks. The earliest forms of "cybercrime" or "hi-tech crime" were conducted by the "phone phreaks" of the 1960s, who discovered ways of overcoming automated phone connection and payment systems in order to make free phone calls. Since the inception of the Internet, the opportunities for cybercrime have increased exponentially. Some forms of cybercrime, such as phishing and fraud, using spam e-mail, will have been encountered by most computer users.

Cybercrimes can be analysed into three types:

(1) the carrying out of conventional crimes using computer technology (this applies to crimes such as fraud, theft, stalking and harassment);

(2) "attack" crimes such as cracking, hacking, releasing viruses and Trojans, and website defacing (the last arguably a hi-tech form of vandalism); and

(3) "content" crimes (such as child pornography and copyright offences).

We will consider some of the main types of cybercrime.

A feature of cybercrimes is that, while they may take a considerable amount of time in preparation, they can be perpetrated extremely fast and may involve a number of different international jurisdictions. This creates considerable problems for investigation and for evidence recovery and retention. The best way to acquire such evidence is by examining the traces left on the perpetrator's or final target's computers. But evidence of crimes may also be recovered by way of data traces left on other computers and servers in the chain of communication.

CONVENTIONAL CRIMES: COMPUTER FRAUD AND IDENTITY THEFT

Films and news reports may lead us to think that computer frauds are perpetrated by organised criminals who hack past firewalls into secure bank computers and transfer huge sums of money into foreign accounts. While these types of organised crime certainly do occur, they are in fact somewhat rare. Most forms of cyber-fraud are carried out by unsophisticated criminals who prey on the laziness, gullibility and greed of the victim. P T Barnum said "There's a sucker born every minute". The most common frauds, often perpetrated by spam e-mail, fall into a large number of well-known categories and are usually simply computer-assisted traditional crimes carried out at low levels of sophistication:

The "area code" scam

This scam plays on people's ignorance of the proliferation of telephone codes. A spammer sends an e-mail (which is now the most common means of starting these crimes) or a fax or letter (but these last two means are not "computer" crimes) which tells the recipient that they have won a prize, a foreign lottery, or some other "too good to be true" offer, and all the recipient has to do is to telephone the sender on their dedicated prize line. The prize line will be a premium number and the recipient unknowingly pays the premium rate while the fraudster profits from this.

The Nigerian (or "advance fee") scam

This scam involves an e-mail message which tells the recipient that the sender is an official in Nigeria or another distant state and that he has a very large some of money which is tied up unexpectedly due to tax or export rules, and needs the help of the recipient as an oversees agent to get the money out of the country. Usually a generous fee of between 10 per cent and 25 per cent will be offered. Once the recipient contacts the scammer, they will be asked for an advance fee to cover initial probate or other expenses. The money is sent and the original spammer is never heard of again.

Pyramid schemes

These schemes tell the recipient of the spam e-mail of a money-making, "get rich quick" scheme which has the same structure as a chain letter: that all the recipient has to do is send some money to a number of addresses at the top of the list sent with the e-mail. The recipient then deletes the top name, moves the other names up one place, adds their own name to the bottom, and then circulates copies to six of their friends who should go through the same steps. Every time someone responds to this scam it increases by six the number of potential victims. Exponential growth of this nature is, of course, utterly impossible and these schemes can do nothing but fail, leaving the victims low down on the list out of pocket. Such scams only benefit those who start such schemes rolling in the first place.

Fraudulent sales

A huge amount of e-mail spam and websites attempt to persuade people to purchase shoddy or non-existent products. Most people will have received spam e-mail purportedly selling Viagra, generic drugs, body enhancement products, miracle health pills and investment products – the list is endless. When victims pay by debit or credit card this has an added dimension to the scam since the victims will have handed over their credit card number and security code which the scammer can use to empty bank accounts or purchase items. Use of card details obtained by fraud to make Internet purchases is sometimes referred to as "card-not-present" fraud.

Phishing

These are clever scams initiated by spam e-mail which appear to be from a bank and ask the recipient to go to a particular website in order to validate their online banking account by putting in their user name and password or update PIN numbers and account details. The site which they tell the recipient to visit will look identical to one from the real bank, even down to the use of that bank's logo and corporate image and to the fact that some of the links from it may take the recipient to links on the bank's real site. The spammer doesn't care if most recipients aren't fooled, since spam e-mails are incredibly cheap and easy to send out in an anonymous multi-mailing. A spammer can send many millions of such e-mails in a day. Even if only one in a million e-mails is responded to by the recipient, it is enough to make the spammer a material profit before the recipient discovers that their account has been emptied. Often spammers will use spiders or bots (small automated search scripts that harvest potential e-mail addresses from the Internet, newsgroups, chat rooms and bulletin boards).

Identity fraud

This occurs when someone obtains access to the victim's personal information such as their name, Social Security number, credit card number or other identifying information and uses these in order to commit fraud or other crimes. This is a variant of the fraudulent and phishing scams, but in this case the scammer uses a stolen identity when they carry out their crimes. People whose identities have been stolen can spend months or years, and a great deal of their hard-earned money, clearing up the mess that identity thieves have made of their name and credit record. In the meantime, victims may lose job opportunities, be refused loans, education, housing or cars, or even be arrested for crimes they did not commit.

Many of these schemes are assisted further by the use of "packet sniffers" or "keystroke loggers" – small programs left on servers or hacked computers aimed at respectively hunting out credit card numbers or recording the keyboard user's user names and passwords which are then sent on automatically to the scammer.

All of the above crimes in this section are well-known traditional crimes and are classified as cybercrimes only because they use computer technology as part of the perpetration method.

"Attack" crimes: "hacking", "cracking" and "denial of service" attacks

"Hackers" and "crackers" are often confused. Both of them try to gain access to other people's computers over the Internet or on a network. They often they do this by breaking through security firewalls or password systems. But sometimes they just look at the contents of an unsecured computer. It is astonishing how many home computer users still do not use a firewall to protect them from intrusion. It is equally astonishing how easy it is to perpetrate these crimes with files and other scripts of very limited sophistication.

Because there is a distinction between protected and unprotected systems, an analogy is sometimes drawn in some jurisdictions between access crimes on computers and the common law crime of housebreaking. If a person sees a house with an open door, walks in, and has a look around inside, they are not committing the crime of housebreaking. However, if they overcome a locked door or break open a window to gain access then they are committing housebreaking. By analogy, in some jurisdictions, for example the USA, access attacks on computers and computer networks may be illegal only when they break through a security system (such as a password system). Where there are no security systems in place then there may be no access crime. In the UK, unauthorised access to computers, a form of unauthorised use of computers, is criminal whether or not a security system is overcome.

Hackers divide themselves between the "good" and the "bad". The "good" hackers (sometimes termed "white hat hackers") regard themselves as people very skilled at using information technology and say they do not intend to do harm to the computers they break into, while the "bad" ("black hat") hackers, who are sometimes also referred to as "crackers", set out to alter data on the computer broken into – often defacing websites and leaving obscenities, uploading viruses and Trojans, or copying and stealing information. Both groups may publicise their successes on hacking and cracking websites. Often, hackers form little mutual support cliques, such as the "Attrition" group of hackers, who set out to attack global businesses which they regard as evil.

Hacking can be conducted by persons with greater or lesser amounts of knowledge and skill. The skilled hackers look down on the "script kiddies" who simply download information about vulnerabilities or hacking tools from hacking websites. It is very easy to find and download these hacking tools and programs which can be used to exploit known vulnerabilities in firewalls and applications. Similarly, hackers may use port-scanning programs which are used to check a range of computers online within particular domains to see if any of their ports are vulnerable and so can provide access to the attached computer.

Since so much business is now conducted over the Internet, hacking can be extremely damaging and costly. Frequently, hackers will facilitate their activities by using small programs called Trojans which can be introduced to a user's computer either by spam e-mail, a document infected by a virus, or the script associated with viewing some websites or image files over the Internet. Trojans, named after the Trojan horse, will sit on the infected computer and open a port so that a hacker can remotely access an infected computer with ease. Often a Trojan will advertise its presence to a known relay which the hacker monitors and thus the hacker comes to know which computers have the Trojan on them and are vulnerable. Such computers can then be attacked or even used as remote servers from which to upload further programs and hence carry out anonymous (from the point of view of the hacker's identity) crimes or attacks such as denial of service attacks on other target computers. Such monitoring of vulnerable computers is now so widespread that a criminal who has the use of a number of infected computers ("bots") may be referred to as a "bot herder".

Denial of service attacks ("DOS attacks") occur where a criminal sends thousands of scripts repeatedly to a target computer ("pinging"). Low-intensity pinging is a normal part of the operation of computer communications systems, however, it is when such pinging is carried out with deliberate repetition and intensity that it constitutes a DOS attack. The effect of a DOS attack is that the target computer is unable to function and becomes slow or useless for as long as the attack continues. DOS attacks are often carried out against target computers owned by organisations disliked by the hacker community or attacks may be conducted by a disgruntled ex-employee or competitor of an online business. The economic effects of a DOS attack can be very severe. DOS attacks can be achieved either by sending scripts from one compromised computer (a "DOS attack") or by using a herd of compromised computers (a "distributed DOS attack"). The latter is much more difficult to investigate since it involves many computers owned by innocent persons who have no idea that their computers have been compromised or used to commit the crime.

All of the above crimes in this section are specific to the information technology environment.

Viruses

Computer viruses are greatly feared by any computer owner since these can destroy all the data on the computer and even render certain computer components permanently useless. They can be very costly to businesses and very distressing to private individuals. Some viruses may replicate and send themselves out to all the names in the target computer's e-mail application. The spread of such multi-mailing viruses is exponential. Sometimes viruses will remain dormant on a computer until the occurrence of a particular event or date at which time they will then become active and will unleash a "payload" with devastating effects. An example of a recent well-known virus was the Melissa virus (the first combination Word macro virus and worm to use the Outlook and Outlook Express address book to send itself to others via e-mail and which appeared in March 1999). Another example is the Trojan.Xombe which first appeared in early 2004 and was sent out to a wide audience. It posed as a message from Microsoft Windows Update, asking subscribers to run an attached revision to Microsoft XP Service Pack 1. What the virus did was "phish" for personal information, passwords or credit card numbers, which information was then sent on to the virus originator. In this way viruses started to become used in economic computer crime.

The typical results of a virus releasing its payload will be a computer slowing to a crawl, strange pictures or messages appearing, computers playing music for no reason, icons on screen moving around automatically and randomly, letters falling to the bottom of the screen, programs failing to load, keyboards not working, times and date stamps on files changing, unknown files appearing and existing files disappearing, hard disks failing to boot, disk drive lights going on for no apparent reason, and so on.

The first computer virus recorded was in 1986 with the "Brain virus" which was first released in Pakistan. Brain Computer Services developed software but it soon fell victim to software piracy as people copied their programs illegally and in contravention of copyright law. The owners of the business decided that people buying pirated copies should be punished for their actions and so they introduced script which was activated when the proprietary software was copied and deleted the boot sectors of the host computer. By today's standards, the Brain virus is rather primitive and things have moved on considerably. It is possible to find and download "virus laboratory" programs from the Internet which enable users to build their own virus out of known sections of script. These tend to be somewhat out of date and are easily recognised and deleted by anti-virus programs. It is interesting to note that most viruses are written for Microsoft Windows operating systems and Microsoft applications.

Almost as harmful as viruses are virus hoaxes which occur when people send spam e-mail warning of some supposedly dangerous file (usually just an innocent part of the computer's operating system) and encouraging the recipients to delete such files and to send a copy of the warning e-mail to all their friends and associates. Such hoaxes cause undue panic and consume huge quantities of Internet bandwidth, thus slowing down or disabling ISPs' services and internet traffic.

Content: child pornography

While the transmission of hardcore pornography is illegal in many countries under obscenity laws (for example, s 2 of the Obscene Publications Act 1959), the most pernicious form of this (and the form which consumes the largest amount of time in terms of detection, investigation and prosecution) is child pornography. This is regulated in Scotland by the Civic Government (Scotland) Act 1982, ss 52 and 52A, as amended by the Protection of Children and Prevention of Sexual Offences (Scotland) Act 2005, s 16 (which together are very similar to s 1 of the Protection of Children Act 1978 (as amended) – the English law equivalent).

The Civic Government (Scotland) Act 1982, ss 52 and 52A (as amended) prohibit the possession, distribution and making of an indecent photograph or pseudo-photograph of a child. A pseudo-photograph is an image which is made to look like a photograph – often by taking, say, the head of a child and invisibly fixing it onto the body of a young-looking adult. What is meant by "indecent" is not defined, but is usually understood to mean that the image shows sexual abuse of the child, nudity, or partial nudity and lewd posing. A "child" is defined as a person under 18 years.

There are statutory defences that a person had a legitimate reason to possess the images (for example, if they seize a computer or disk containing the images for the purposes of handing them over to the police) or that the person had not himself seen the images and did not know or have any cause to suspect the images to be indecent (such as where background images may be automatically downloaded from websites, pop-ups or spam e-mail, and retained in a computer's cache memory). The essence of "possession" is that the person possessing has both knowledge and control over the images.

Clearly, making or distributing an indecent image of a child is much more serious. These crimes may incur a maximum penalty of 10 years' imprisonment and entry on the Sex Offenders Register. The range of sentencing options and policy is now greatly assisted by the English Sentencing Advisory Panel's guidelines which analyse factors, including the type of indecent image concerned, which provide definition as to the seriousness of the criminal's conduct. No such sentencing guidelines exist yet in Scotland. The guidelines are a very good example of the way that relatively simple offences, legally speaking, can involve complex sentencing rules – of course, the guidelines are English, but in practice similar principles are applied in Scotland.

The most recent notorious example of a UK child pornography investigation was Operation Ore in which the FBI and the US postal service provided the names of 7,500 people living in the UK who had used credit cards to access the Landslide pornography portal in Texas. Of these, around 1,200 people were arrested and over the last 3 years a significant number of those arrested have been successfully convicted of possession and distribution of images found on their computers following raids of their homes. The biggest difficulty in the fight against child pornography is that much of the Internet is effectively unregulated and many child pornography sites are located in jurisdictions beyond usual controls, such as in Russia, Ukraine, Malaysia and other far Eastern countries.

STATUTORY SOLUTIONS: THE COMPUTER MISUSE ACT 1990 (AS AMENDED)

No new statutory solutions are required to deal with crimes which are merely perpetrated using computer technology. However, access-type and content-type computer crimes require express statutory solutions.

The Computer Misuse Act 1990 ("CMA") was an early attempt to criminalise types of unlawful computer activity. While the Act has been amended by the Police and Justice Act 2006, the CMA remains the principal statute criminalising computer and hi-tech crimes in the UK. Over the years, it has proved remarkably effective despite its simplicity.

The CMA (as amended) creates four offences in ss 1–3A. These are respectively:

Unauthorised access to computer material (s 1)

It is an offence to cause a computer to perform any function with intent to gain unauthorised access to any program or data held in any computer. This offence requires proof of two elements of *mens rea*: the intention to access the program or data held on the target computer, and knowledge that the access was unauthorised. The classic example of this offence is hacking.

Unauthorised access to computer material with intent to commit or facilitate commission of further offences (s 2)

This offence is committed when the facts are the same as in s 1, except that, in this case, the crime is committed with the intention of committing or facilitating the commission of a further offence. Even if it is not possible to prove intent to commit the further offence, the offence of simple unauthorised access (s 1) is still committed as a statutory alternative, provided that both elements of the *mens rea* are proved.

Unauthorised acts with intent to impair or hinder the operation of a computer (s 3)

This offence is committed if any person carries out an unauthorised act with intent to impair the operation of a computer or with intent to hinder access to, or impair the operation of, any program or data on a computer. The accused must have the intent to cause the hindering or impairment and know that the act is authorised. There is no necessity for any unauthorised access to have been obtained during the commission of this offence. This means that a person who has authorised access to a computer may nevertheless still be liable under this section if he deliberately carries out an act with intent to impair or hinder. In addition to criminalising damage to or theft of data caused by hackers, this offence is intended to include denial of service attacks. The definition also includes distributing viruses and Trojans which are clearly intended to impair the operation of computers.

Making, supplying or obtaining articles for use in computer misuse offences (s 3A)

While ss 1–3 (as amended) deal with most categories of computer crime, the use of port sniffers, packet sniffers for the interception of communications, writing and distribution of viruses and Trojans, and certain other categories of hi-tech crime present difficulties of categorisation. Some of these issues are now dealt with by s 3A which is intended to criminalise the making, supplying or obtaining of any article intending that it should be used for the commission of any of the previous three offences. This offence clearly prevents the trade and distribution of viruses, Trojans and other malicious forms of script where the requisite malicious intent is involved. But, at the same time, the section is carefully worded to allow computer industry specialists to make, supply and obtain such scripts and programs which may have dual uses for lawful purposes, such as the testing, maintenance and development of computer networks and security systems.

An interesting and somewhat unusual example of a prosecution under CMA, s 1 occurred in the case of *Director of Public Prosecutions* v *Bignall* (1998). This case involved officers serving in the Metropolitan Police. The first respondent left his wife to live with the second respondent and a dispute arose concerning two motor cars owned by a Mr Howells, the new partner of the first respondent's former wife. On six occasions during December 1994 and March and May 1995, the respondents instructed police computer operators to extract from the Police National Computer (PNC) details of the registration and ownership of the two motor cars. They were charged with six offences contrary to s 1, in that they had gained unauthorised access to the PNC. The two respondents, as serving police officers, were entitled to access to the PNC on a daily basis in the course of their duties, for the lawful purposes of their employment, but their access of the same resource for personal purposes was not authorised. Authorised access to the PNC is confidential and for police operational use only. A person who does not have access at the appropriate level commits an offence if he accesses the computer beyond that authority, either by doing so himself or by getting someone else to do so for him, even if the latter had authority to access the computer and was unaware that the access asked of them was unauthorised.

The Cybercrime Treaty

The Council of Europe passed a Convention on Cybercrime in November 2001 (the "Cybercrime Treaty"). The United Kingdom was one of the 25 or so signatories to the Convention. The most important provisions comprise an analysis of different forms of hi-tech crime which are already effectively criminalised in the UK.

The main difference between the Cybercrime Treaty and the CMA (as amended) is that the former is much more specific and detailed (which reflected the much more detailed experience of hi-tech crime during the intervening 11-year period).

Articles 2–6 deal with illegal access to computer systems, illegal interception of non-public transmissions of computer data (eg e-mails), data and system interference, and the misuse of technological devices and programs (including the production, sale, procuring, import or distribution of devices or programs) for use to commit any of the previous offences. This group of offences may be analysed as access, confidentiality and integrity offences. Articles 7 and 8 deal with computer related forgery and fraud. Articles 9 and 10 deal with the content crimes of child pornography and copyright offences.

Some people object to the Cybercrime Treaty on the basis that it was written by bureaucrats and so does not strike a fair balance between the public interest in criminalising and enforcing cybercrimes and fundamental individual rights to privacy and personal data protection. Particular areas of concern are Arts 25–28 which comprise the General Principles relating to Mutual Assistance in which signatory states agree to allow the development of informal as well as formal contact between investigative bodies and the informal and formal sharing of information and intelligence which results. There have been a number of problems with this. For example, there is frequently too much reliance on informal sharing of what is really confidential personal and sensitive personal data about citizens. Also, there is often a mis-match between the standards and protocols of evidence collection between different signatory states (and even between what is legal or illegal in the different signatory states). These problems, together with problems of evidential quality and integrity, have marred several prominent cybercrime investigations. For example, in one case the FBI prepared informal lists of "suspects" in surveillance operations and provided these to UK police who then used this information as though the lists held the names of "suspects" as the expression is understood under UK laws (where suspects are not regarded as such unless there are reasonable and often corroborated grounds for suspicion that the named persons have or are committing crimes).

In addition, many of the Treaty's objectives have proved to be impracticable, such as the suggestion that signatories should be able to issue "retention orders" that would freeze data on any computer or network of computers in real time and capture all the data traffic on the computers and network – including the content of any communications. This is theoretically possible, but at present would be very costly in terms of money and computing power. In addition, the capture of communication content (the whole information content of communications) rather than merely traffic data (that is records of which computer sent data to which other computer, how much data (in terms of size and type) was sent, and when was the data sent, but where the information content of the data is not recorded), may contravene the standards of privacy expected in civilised states. Usually the only time when content of communications can be gathered lawfully is where a court warrant or formal order has been obtained when specific suspects have been identified. Bureaucrats should surely not have power to do this without supervision?

New areas of cybercrime: cyberstalking and "grooming"

At the moment there is no universally accepted definition of cyber-stalking, and the term is used to referred to the use of Internet, e-mail and other electronic communications devices in order to stalk or harass another person. Such stalking generally involves harassing or threatening behaviour that an individual engages in repeatedly, such as following a person, appearing at a person's home or place of business, making harassing phone calls, leaving written messages or objects, or vandalising a person's property. Most "real-world stalking" laws require that the perpetrator makes a credible threat of violence against the victim, but some include also the threats against the victim's immediate family, while others require merely that the stalker's course of conduct constitutes an implied threat.

Cyberstalking is based on the analogy with the real world but the harassing or threatening behaviour is conducted over the Internet. One example of cyberstalking which has been in the news recently is the online "stalking" and "grooming" of children in Internet chat rooms. The Government has recently issued guidelines to reduce the risk of paedophiles making contact with minors in online chat rooms, establishing relationships with children in order that they may later make contact for the purpose of engaging in criminal sexual activities. However, cyberstalking, is not limited to predation upon children but can include a whole range of harassing and threatening behaviours and types of intended victim. When we look at the analogy between real-world stalking and cyberstalking, a number of striking differences can be seen: first, real-world stalking generally requires the perpetrator and victim to be present in the same geographical area, while cyberstalkers may be located across the street or across the country or even abroad; second, electronic communication technologies make it easy for a cyberstalker to engage third parties to harass and/or threaten the victim (one example is where a person mimics the victim in a bulletin board or chat room and posts inflammatory messages which may damage the reputation of the victim and result in the victim being "flamed" or sent viruses by a large number of online objectors); and, third, electronic communication technologies also lower the barriers to harassments and threats because a cyberstalker does not need physically to confront the victim. In Scotland, cyberstalking can be prosecuted as a form of breach of the peace, a common law crime.

There are now specific provisions aimed at criminalising child "grooming". The Protection of Children and Prevention of Sexual Offences (Scotland) Act 2005 (Sexual Offences Act 2003 in England) makes it a crime to befriend a child on the Internet, or indeed by any other means, and thereafter to meet or intend to meet the child with the intention of abusing them.

Cybercrime evidence and jurisdictional issues

Perhaps the most constraining factor relation to all cybercrime is the question of the gathering of evidence. This is intertwined with the difficulties of jurisdiction.

In any communication by e-mail or over the Internet, between the originating and recipient computers there is a long chain of intermediate computers. For example, when an e-mail is sent, the e-mail will be automatically disassembled, packeted, transmitted and re-assembled on each of the computers in the chain. This means that there is scope for a number of different jurisdictions to be involved. For example, if a UK sender uses AOL as their Internet Service Provider and a UK recipient uses CompuServe, it is likely that the e-mail will be distributed via computer relays in the United States. So geographical location is a complicating factor in cybercrime and it follows that international jurisdictions will be involved. This complicates the gathering of evidence of criminal activity.

Equally complicating is the fact that cybercrimes can be completed in an instant. This means that investigating agencies are very anxious to acquire as much traffic (and where possible content) information as possible (balancing this with the rights of individuals to privacy). But traffic information is rarely retained on servers for long and content information is particularly volatile.

The best evidence of the commission of crimes would still appear to be that which is recoverable from dawn raids on suspects' houses and the seizure of suspects' computers. Such equipment can then be subjected to computer forensic testing to see what incriminating evidence can be recovered even after it has been deleted. Forensic computer techniques vary in sophistication but can consume costly resources in terms of time, expense and use of computer facilities. The more serious the cybercrime, the more sophisticated the forensic techniques that can be justified.

An increasingly common difficulty encountered is the use of strong encryption techniques such as PGP ("pretty good privacy" – a now very common and easily available encryption technique). Encrypted hard disks and data are very difficult and costly to decrypt, rendering much computer evidence inaccessible. Yet another difficulty is that it is now very easy to carry out secure deletion of incriminating data. All of these problems renders cybercrime detection, investigation and prosecution a very challenging and rapidly evolving area of law.

The Regulation of Investigatory Powers Acts

Another way of obtaining evidence of crimes is by obtaining a warrant to carry out surveillance. This area is now regulated by the Regulation of Investigatory Powers Act 2000 ("RIPA") and the Regulation of Investigatory Powers (Scotland) Act 2000 ("RIPSA") which are broadly similar except that RIPSA is restricted to the general conduct of surveillance while RIPA deals with a number of very specific areas and gives the UK Government very wide powers to authorise surveillance.

Both Acts set out the conditions upon which directed, intrusive or human intelligence may be authorised and carried out to pursue investigations with the broad aims of preventing crime and disorder, in the interests of public safety or for the protection of public health. The Acts ensure that all levels of surveillance are authorised at a level appropriate for the type of surveillance involved and that there is maintained a balance between the public interests involved and private privacy and confidentiality. Government Ministers (the Scottish Ministers in Scotland) are required to issue codes of practice relating to the conduct of surveillance. Authorisations of surveillance operations are subject to supervision by judicial surveillance commissioners who have the power to quash authorisations and destroy records. There is provision for appeal against a surveillance commissioner's actions. In addition, an "aggrieved person" may appeal against the conduct of a surveillance operation to the Regulation of Investigatory Powers Tribunal set up for this purpose.

Complaints have to be made within 1 year (RIPA, s 67(5)) and in most cases the subjects of surveillance operations will not know that they have been subject to such surveillance and so that they have such rights.

It has been suggested that RIPA allows the UK Government powers to access a person's electronic communications in a relatively unrestricted manner, thus infringing the privacy of an individual's correspondence in a manner that many would not tolerate if it applied to their postal communications. In particular, RIPA enables the UK Government to demand that an ISP provides secret access to a customer's communications on the authority of an "interception warrant" (RIPA, s 8). The justification for such warrants include national security, the prevention or detection of serious crime, or the safeguarding of the economic wellbeing of the UK. Not only can the Home Secretary serve interception warrants to examine the communications of named individual persons and premises, but warrants can be issued to collect all external communications of an ISP or telecommunications service on the basis of the same "justification". The UK Government is empowered to require ISPs to fit surveillance equipment.

The UK Government has broad powers to demand individuals to hand over decryption keys in order to enable Government access to encrypted information (RIPA, s 49). A failure to hand over such a key is an offence punishable by up to 2 years' imprisonment (RIPA, s 53). Any person who has ever had such a key at any stage in their possession is deemed under RIPA to possess it for an indefinite period, and a person does not cease to be under an obligation to hand over such a key even if the key has been lost or forgotten about years before. This power appears to be both disproportionate in effect and also in many cases impossible to comply with, as encryption keys may be created automatically by computer programs and the user of such programs may be utterly unaware that such keys exist. Many websites secure communications using such automatic encryption technology (for example, Amazon's "shopping basket" or account log-in). A number of similar administrative powers additionally may be associated with a demand that any order made is kept secret by the person to whom the order is made, and it is an offence for such a person to reveal that such an order has been made. The penalty for this offence is a maximum of 5 years' imprisonment.

At the time when RIPA was passed there was a considerable amount of contrary opinion as to its efficacy and proportionality. It has been said that RIPA also includes a power which allows the Home Secretary to authorise officials to access Internet traffic data without a warrant for any reason which the Home Secretary sees fit, subject to parliamentary approval. The complaint is that this power effectively means that citizens can be put under surveillance for any reason whatsoever. It is envisaged that the State can gather information about what websites individuals have visited and when, what e-mails are sent and received, what newsgroups a person reads, the phone numbers a person calls, what software or documents a person downloads, where and when a citizen logs onto a computer and from where, etc. The only balancing check on this power would appear to be that such surveillance data cannot yet be used in most legal proceedings – though the reasons for this have nothing to do with individual privacy and freedoms but are justified by the need to keep government sources and surveillance techniques and procedures secret. It was suggested that RIPA was neither an acceptable nor a responsible means of achieving the goals of public safety, that the Act would inhibit the development of the Internet and e-commerce, that it would create a range of onerous and unfair impositions on individuals, organisations and companies, particularly in restricting their rights of privacy and freedom of expression, and in the costs incurred, and that it substantially centralised powers and increased the powers of law enforcement and security agencies without providing adequate measures for authorisation and supervision. It was also felt that the ability of government to demand decryption keys created a dangerous precedent which would affect the rights of all computer users, and that the surveillance of websites would undermine confidence in the Internet as a means of communication. The Government was urged to ensure that a fair balance of interests was struck and that any measures adopted should not violate the rights to liberty, fair trial, freedom of expression, freedom of association, and privacy (most of the above objections were expressed in a letter to the *Daily Telegraph* of 12 July 2000 which had 49 notable signatories from many prominent and influential persons and organisations). However, it has to be said that, in the period since then, it has not produced as many damaging situations as had been predicted.

Essential Facts

- Cybercrimes, or "hi-tech" crimes, are crimes committed using computer technology. Such crimes may be analysed into three types: (1) traditional crimes carried out using computer technology, such as computer fraud; (2) "attack" crimes such as hacking or releasing viruses and Trojans, and "denial of service" attacks; and (3) content crimes such as child pornography or criminalised copyright offences.

- The Computer Misuse Act 1990 (as amended) creates four crimes which cover most forms of computer crime:
    - s 1 makes it a crime to obtain unauthorised access to a computer or to any program or data held on any computer. This section therefore covers hacking and similar offences;
    - s 2 makes it a crime to obtain unauthorised access to a computer or a program of data held on a computer in order to commit any further offence;
    - s 3 makes it a crime to carry out any unauthorised acts in order to impair or hinder the operation of a computer. This section covers damage or theft caused by hackers, the releasing of viruses and Trojans, and "denial of service" attacks;
    - s 3A makes it a crime to make supply of obtain articles for use in computer misuse offences. This section is aimed at preventing the trade and distribution of articles including programs for use in computer crime.

- Child pornography is criminalised under the Civic Government (Scotland) Act 1982, ss 52 and 52A (as amended) which makes it a crime to make, possess or distribute indecent photographs of children.

- Cyberstalking, consisting of harassing and threatening behaviour carried out using computers, is covered by the common law crime of breach of the peace.

- The Protection of Children and Prevention of Sexual Offences (Scotland) Act 2005 makes it a crime to "groom" children for sexual purposes over the Internet.

- The Council of Europe's Cybercrime Treaty dated November 2001 laid out provisions which enabled cybercrimes to be harmonised among signatory states and also set up General Principles relating to Mutual Assistance allowing formal and informal co-operation among law enforcement bodies in signatory states. Differing standards among the signatory states have led to a number of notable problems.

- The investigating and collection of evidence of cybercrime is a challenging area of law enforcement. Cybercrimes may involve a number of international jurisdictions, they may be completed in an instant, evidence on servers may be volatile in the sense of overwritten or deleted automatically in a very short period. The best evidence is usually obtained by the lawful seizure of a perpetrator's computer. Computer forensic techniques can recover deleted data.

- Another means of gathering evidence of computer crime is by means of surveillance techniques regulated under the Regulation of Investigatory Powers Act 2000 and the Regulation of Investigatory Powers (Scotland) Act 2000. These Acts set out the conditions whereby directed, intrusive or human surveillance may be carried out, with appropriate authorisations, and subject to the supervision of surveillance commissioners. Aggrieved parties may make a complaint to the Regulation of Investigatory Powers Tribunal. RIPA contains wide powers to allow surveillance of computer communications, the recovery of encryption keys, and creates a number of offences. RIPA in particular has had a bad press but few scare stories have proved justified by events.

Essential Case

Director of Public Prosecutions v Bignall (1998): this case involved two officers serving in the Metropolitan Police who accessed the Police National Computer (PNC) to obtain information about the ownership of two vehicles. They were charged with six offences under s 1 of the Computer Misuse Act 1990 in that they had gained unauthorised access to the PNC. They were entitled to access the PNC on a daily basis in the course of their duties for the lawful purposes of their employment but their access of the same resource for personal purposes was not authorised.

INDEX